Bibliographic information published by the German National Library:

The German National Library lists this publication in the National Bibliography; detailed bibliographic data are available on the Internet at http://dnb.dnb.de .

Imprint:

Copyright © 2017 GRIN Verlag
Print and binding: Books on Demand GmbH, Norderstedt Germany
ISBN: 9783668830011

This book at GRIN:

https://www.grin.com/document/446484

James Khan

A Study in Protocol Obfuscation Techniques and their Effectiveness

GRIN Verlag

GRIN - Your knowledge has value

Since its foundation in 1998, GRIN has specialized in publishing academic texts by students, college teachers and other academics as e-book and printed book. The website www.grin.com is an ideal platform for presenting term papers, final papers, scientific essays, dissertations and specialist books.

A Study in Protocol Obfuscation Techniques and their Effectiveness

James Khan

2017

Kellogg College
University of Oxford

A dissertation submitted for the
MSc in Software and Systems Security

Abstract

There are two main reasons for people to hide their network communication. Some want to maintain their privacy, while others need to access resources that might not be available to them due to restrictions applied by a censor.

Monitoring of internet usage by the governments is not something new but now many countries have actively started blocking internet content for their citizens. Necessity is the mother of invention. Researchers and developers are working on ingenious ways of bypassing such monitoring and restrictions.

In recent years, protocol obfuscation is becoming a burning topic especially because of evolution of some state level censors. Internet users want to freely access resources however censors are deployed by several countries around to world to restrict this access. As the protocol obfuscation techniques are gradually improving and so are the censors.

Meanwhile, there are some internet users who do not live in countries that restrict their access to the internet resources in any way but these individuals are concerned about confidentiality of their internet use. Government agencies are frequently in the media over accusations of spying, on their own citizens as well as citizens of other countries, which is making many internet users alarmed about their anonymity.

Both censors and circumvention tools are evolving continuously and gradually. The aim of this study was to analyse the protocol obfuscation techniques and systems available to ordinary internet users. The efficiency of these techniques and systems is assessed in the light of available research in respect of detecting obfuscated protocols. Once a research proves that an obfuscation technique can be successfully attacked it makes it easier to implement possible mitigations and the research also provides guidance to the developers of future protocol obfuscation systems so that they learn from the mistakes of others. It was noted that all the protocol obfuscation systems researched in this study are vulnerable to detection. In some cases, the detection does not even require the use of sophisticated resources.

The author confirms that: this dissertation does not contain material previously submitted for another degree or academic award; and the work presented here is the author's own, except where otherwise stated.

Table of Contents

1. Introduction

Internet users can utilise protocol obfuscation for circumventing censorship, or anonymity and confidential browsing. Potentially any protocol can be obfuscated but the most commonly obfuscated protocols are http, https, video, and voice, including some propriety protocols.

According to the Oxford Dictionary obfuscation means "the action of making something obscure, unclear, or unintelligible" [43]. The concept of obfuscation is not something new. Soldiers and fighters have been using paint for thousands of years for camouflage and for making themselves obscure [44]. In the World War II, planes used to drop black paper with aluminium foil at the back to trick the radar into thinking that there are too many planes in the sky; hence, hiding the location of the actual plane in the noise [42].

Internet censorship and surveillance is a well-known problem in many countries. Moreover, there are 19 countries named "Enemies of the Internet" by the Reporters San Frontieres or Reporters without Borders [32]. These countries include Bahrain, USA, Syria, United Arab Emirates, Cuba, Iran, United Kingdom, Uzbekistan, India, Pakistan, China, North Korea, Vietnam, Turkmenistan, Belarus, Russia, Sudan, Saudi Arabia, and Ethiopia [32].

In March 2013, Iranian authorities blocked non-government registered VPN services to block access to the censored material [17]. Great Firewall of China blocks Facebook, Twitter, and some well-known news websites like Reuters, Wall Street Journal and BBC Chinese as reported by ProPublica [27]. The Great Firewall uses different methods for blocking the user access including DNS Poisoning, IP address blocking, analysing and filtering URLs, packet inspection and filtering, man-in-the-middle attack, TCP connection reset, network enumeration, and blocking VPN connections [28].

Some Chinese users have used different methods for bypassing the Great Firewall in the past but as the firewall is evolving it is becoming harder and harder to bypass the restrictions imposed by the censor. Initially, VPN was an obvious choice but in 2011 the users reported that the VPN connections were unstable and in 2012 the

VPN services were completely blocked [20]. Some users turned to the Tor network for anonymity and for bypassing the firewall but later, as described by Moghaddam et al. [18], the Great Firewall also started blocking the Tor Relays, which are publicly listed. As a solution, the Tor project implemented bridges which provide interface to the Tor network and unlike relays are not publicly listed [18].

"Privacy intrusions have both epistemic and psychological components, and can range in value from relatively trivial considerations to those of profound consequence for an individual's dignity, integrity, and autonomy" [46].

For several countries, including the western democracies, encryption has become a serious issue when encryption is used by terrorists for communication with each other and for planning attacks. After the March 2017 terrorist attack in Westminster London, the BBC reported that two minutes before the attack the attacker was using WhatsApp, which provides end to end encrypted communication [5]. BBC gave details in the news article that police could not read the terrorist's messages and quoted the UK home secretary Amber Rudd saying that "there must be 'no place for terrorists to hide' and intelligence services must have access to encrypted messaging services" [5].

Brunton and Nissenbaum [42] define obfuscation as "deliberate addition of ambiguous, confusing, or misleading information to interfere with surveillance and data collection". Whether for confidential browsing or circumventing censorship of a repressive regime, privacy is becoming a major concern for many. Censorship circumvention and confidential browsing systems that use protocol obfuscation are deemed quite effective at the time of creation but very soon become redundant because either a research proves that the obfuscation can be traced or users report that the system is no longer effective. Evidence suggests that within a year or two, if not a lot sooner, either the network protocol obfuscation system is successfully attacked in an academic research or by a censor leaving the system useless or the system is not practical and did not get enough traction and fame among the users. Therefore, the protocol obfuscation systems become deprecated very soon, for example, in the case of browser proxies which in theory is a very good concept but for the system to be an effective censorship circumvention tool it requires a large number of internet users to use browser proxies and as it did not happen the project was unsuccessful nearly from the start. However, Brunton and Nissenbaum [42] describe this dilemma in a different way. They say that obfuscation works and is useful even if it lives for a short while because sometimes obfuscation is required only for a short while [42]. However, most of the time citizens of oppressed regimes require uncensored access to the internet for an unlimited period of time. A considerable amount of research is underway for both improving privacy of internet users and censor circumvention. However, on the other hand efforts, resources, and a great deal of investment is going into the improvements of censors and the new ways in which censors and government security agencies around the world are collecting internet users' data. Most of the research on protocol obfuscation is performed by universities and in some cases volunteers. There is some evidence of research done and systems produced by large organisations but their intentions are hard to guess i.e. whether they are doing this for the better good of the internet freedom or for their own hidden agendas. For example, volunteers and students write Pluggable Transports for Tor. The life span of most systems is very small because the information about how these systems work is generally available on the internet to everyone. In most cases, creators of the systems write papers or guidelines about how the system works. There are advantages of writing these papers but one prominent disadvantage is that as soon as a censorship circumvention system becomes popular it gets blocked by the censors.

Another notable fact about the use of censorship circumvention systems is that they are not easy to install and configure. A large majority of ordinary internet users are not tech savvy. UX or User Experience of many software applications and website is improving. Tor browser is easy to install and use however, some Pluggable Transport for Tor are not easy to install and configure. Therefore, it makes it difficult for an ordinary internet user to take advantage of these inventions. An anonymous internet user from China mentioned that the speed of Tor is slow and the technical knowledge required for operating Tor as a user[1] needs to be high.

This study discusses several methods and tools for protocol obfuscation that are available to ordinary users. Some tools are designed for circumventing internet censorship while others are more specifically created for confidential browsing. Goals of a successful protocol masquerade process are also presented in this paper.

---

[1] See Appendix B1 – Comments about Tor from Chinese Users.

This study describes what systems are freely available to general public and collates flaws in those systems in a single piece of documentation. It will help in design and development of better and more sophisticated protocol masquerade systems in the future.

This introduction is the first section of the dissertation. The second section provides the background of the internet censorship and internet user anonymity problem. The third section of the dissertation covers the applications of network protocol obfuscation, the types of protocol obfuscation systems available freely on the internet, description of traffic morphing, and most importantly the goals of a successful protocol masquerade process. The fourth section discusses the protocol masquerade systems (systems that provide both protocol obfuscation and traffic morphing) in detail. In the fifth section research on detecting the traffic generated by the protocol obfuscation systems is discussed. Sixth section discusses and argues the analysis presented in the study and the seventh section proposes future work. The eighth section concludes the study.

2. Background

As the censorship circumvention systems are improving and so are the censors. As we will establish in this paper, censorship circumvention systems which seem effective when they are launched become ineffective very soon. The reason is the constant evolution of the censors. Some countries like China are on the forefront of this battle. China built the Great Firewall (GFW) with the help of Fang Binxing who is commonly known as the Father of GFW [39]. There is no definitive figure on the cost of building or running the GFW. However, according to one rumour, by 2002 China had spent an estimated $770 million on its internet censor technology [37]. More than one hundred of the top one thousand world's most popular websites are blocked in China [41].

The requirement for internet censor circumvention mechanisms was born when countries started monitoring the internet use of their citizens, some began to restrict access to certain internet resource, and some organisations also started blocking internet access to some websites and services.

Countries monitor and restrict access for several reasons. Chances of terrorism may be high in a country and therefore the security agencies of the country feel a need to monitor or block internet access to certain sources. Some countries block internet access during civil unrest or during war to keep control over their citizens and regulate the information flow. In some cases, laws of a country may dictate that the internet access to and/or from certain locations should be blocked, monitored, governed, and/or restricted. A country may monitor or block internet access to avoid the spread of propaganda created by its enemies.

Networks in most large organisations are monitored and in many cases access to some websites is restricted when employees are using the organisational network. In most cases, this is to monitor and block leaking of confidential organisation information and business secrets, adherence to organisational and industry regulations, and making sure employees do not waste time on non-official activities like browsing social media when at work. A news report published by The Wall Street Journal revealed that some senior executives believe in monitoring the internet use of their employees while others are against it and find such an effort damaging [89].

It is acknowledged that monitoring and restrictions on the free internet use are in place. It is not the purpose of this study to evaluate whether such restrictions on the free use of internet are valid or not. The study is agnostic of the geo-political situations and governing laws. The study covers the technology aspect of censorship circumvention to the unrestricted and free internet and avoidance of monitoring of the internet use.

1. Problem Domain

The purpose of protocol obfuscation is to confuse the observer about the type of protocol that is actually being transmitted over a medium. Therefore, if the observer can, with a certain degree of accuracy and confidence, detect that a protocol is being obfuscated then the objective of the obfuscation is unsuccessful.

Several tools and techniques will be discussed in this paper along with analysis of research done in this field that will help identify if a particular obfuscation system can be successfully detected or not.

1.1. Internet Censor Timeline

Here is a timeline of some key events in the context of internet monitoring, restrictions on free internet use, internet attacks, protocol obfuscation and traffic morphing.

Major Events

Aug 1996	Several well-known websites are blocked in China; these sites included Voice of America, and human-rights and Western news groups [36].
Jun 1997	Term "The Great Firewall of China" is first used in a Wired magazine article [40].
Aug 2002	Design of Infranet, a censorship circumvention system, is revealed [84].
Sep 2002	The onion routing network is put into practice for the first time [48].

Sep 2002	Google is blocked in China for the first time [36].
2003	Information about Golden Shield Project is one of China's highly guarded state secrets. There is varying information about when the Golden Shield Project started. According to Radio Free Asia [15] it started in 2003. While, The Atlantic reported that the project started in May 2001 [37].
Nov 2006	Golden shield project part 1 starts operating [21].
2006	Internet censorship comes into force in Saudi Arabia by their Communications and Information Technology Commission [33].
Mar 2008	YouTube is blocked in China [36].
Feb 2009	Wright, C., Coulls, S., and Monrose, F. [9] propose traffic morphing.
Jul 2009	Facebook and Twitter are blocked in China [36].
2011	GreatFire.org a non-profit organisation that advocates against Internet censorship in China starts [26].
Mar 2012	Pakistani authorities published a public tender for building an internet censor similar to the Great Firewall of China [16, 31].
Jun-Oct 2012	Bloomberg and New York Times websites are blocked in China [36].
Nov 2012	Lenta.ru reports [34] that Russian authorities started blocking several websites.
July 2014	Das Erste, a publically owned German television channel, discovers that a server in Germany containing Tor node and directory authority is under surveillance by the US intelligence organisation NSA [86].
Dec 2015	Russians seek help from China for building a censor system similar to the Great Firewall [39].
Nov 2016	Russia blocks access to LinkedIn [38].
Jan 2017	China blocks several China based VPN service providers [41].

May 2017	Ukraine implements sanctions on Russian businesses by blocking some of country's most famous websites because they are owned by Russian companies [78].
Jun 2017	Egypt blocks 100 websites including some Al Jazeera websites and HuffPost Arabic [77].
Jul 2017	From the beginning of 2018 China to start blocking VPNs that have not been authorised by the government [72, 73, 76].
Jul 2017	Apple removes apps that help circumvent the Great Firewall from their App Store [75].
Jul 2017	China blocks photo, voice, and video messages sent on WhatsApp [74].
Jul 2017	It is reported that China is to launch world's first network, called the Jinan network, using quantum technology where attacks on the network communication will be detectable [71].

1.2. Tor Detection by the Great Firewall

Protocol Obfuscation plays a big part in free movement of information over the internet without obstructions. Free movement of information over the internet is considered a cat and mouse game played by the security researchers, internet users, and the nation states who want to restrict users from freely accessing the internet. The reality is that it is not a cat and mouse game anymore. Censors like the Great Firewall are far ahead in the game. China has the technical capability, investment, and laws to stop its internet users from accessing blocked internet content.

Winter and Crandall [30] explained that the Tor clients download information about the Tor relays during the bootstrapping process from the published Tor directories. Winter and Crandall also observed that Tor developers implemented unpublished relays called bridges to overcome the problem of blocking of published relays [30]. However, the bridges created another problem as described by Winter and Crandall. "In an ideal world bridges should only be given to censored users, a censor can always mimic users and obtain — and then block — bridges the same way. The current approach to the bridge distribution problem is to make it easy to

get some of them but hard to get all of them because then a censor could simply block them all. While the public network was blocked at this point in China, bridges remained functioning and were used heavily.
The increasing popularity of bridges did not remain unnoticed, though. Several months later, in March 2010, the Chinese bridge usage statistics started to drop significantly" [30].

Winter and Crandall [30] observed that censorship evasion systems including Tor can be blocked by either detecting and blocking by traffic signatures of the protocol or by simply harvesting relays and bridges.

Winter and Crandall [30] also noted the work of Fifield et al. [22] on flash proxies. The concept "turns web site visitors outside the censoring regime into short-lived stepping stones into the Tor network. The short-livedness is an advantage as well as a disadvantage. The disadvantage is that long-lived TCP connections can get terminated frequently. The advantage is that the mere volume of web site visitors can be too much for a blacklist to handle. The censor should get overwhelmed by the amount of end points to block and discontinue blacklisting." [30].

Wang et al. [2] quoted the work of Winter and Crandall [30] on how the Great Firewall of China blocks Tor by using a "two-stage detection pipeline" to increase precision. In the first stage the Great Firewall, "uses DPI to flag flows as potentially resulting from a censorship circumvention tool" and in the second stage the destination IP addresses of these flagged flows are analysed for Tor handshake using a Tor client [2].

2. Methods and Systems

Researchers are considering different ways of circumventing censorship. Protocol Obfuscation is one of the ways. There are several other ways, for example, Telex [59], Cirripede [79] and Decoy Routing [80] which rely on a co-operation by the ISPs as observed by Moghaddam [8]. These systems are out of the context of this study as the scope is to analyse protocol obfuscation systems and techniques.

This study considers different protocol obfuscation techniques and systems, and existing research into detecting these particular protocol obfuscations. In recent years, several systems have been designed and implemented for evading censorship and improving confidential browsing. However, Moghaddam noted that extraordinary efficiency and speed is still not achieved in the obfuscation systems [8].

Several threat models are discussed in this study but most are very simple. The adversary is usually a state-run censor and firewalls, or state owned monitoring systems. Monitoring systems are passive and do not block traffic while censors and firewalls are usually reactive and block traffic if they detect unusual behaviour or transmission of censored content. The adversary is supposed to have abundance of resources available and it can manipulate traffic easily. It can flag and reroute suspected traffic to dedicated channels for an in-depth investigation.

3. Protocol Obfuscation

The term Protocol Obfuscation was first used in eMule [19]. According to eMule, protocol obfuscation technology can shield its traffic and can create misguidance by concealing its protocol [19].

1. Applications of Network Protocol Obfuscation

Following are some scenarios where protocol obfuscation can be used for achieving censorship circumvention, confidentiality, or anonymity.

1.1. Web Browsing

A user may choose protocol obfuscation for web browsing as a means for evading censorship or achieving confidential browsing. Several solutions are discussed in §4 for evading censors. The censors may be imposed by nation states, ISPs, or organizations. Nation states enforce internet censors for several reasons some of which may be political, religious, repression of freedom of speech, or control over e-commerce. Internet Service Providers restrict their users from visiting certain websites or using certain protocol because of internal policies and local or national government regulations. Organizations employ censors to improve their security and to implement their policies.

Solutions
Obfs4, meek, FTE, etc.

1.2. Emails

Some nation states have strict policies about sending emails outside the country. Some states are at war and monitor all communications. An internet user may need protocol obfuscation for anonymity or censor circumvention. Such a user might be a reporter or someone who wants to convey her opinion outside the state. This user's opinion could be contrary to the government's ambitions. If detected, emails of such a user may get blocked or the user can even find herself in a difficult situation with the authorities. For such a user evading censorship without detection would be a high priority.

There are several email encryption systems available but a user may want to not only encrypt the emails but also obfuscate the network protocol to avoid detection.

Solutions
StegoTorus, FreeWave, SkypeMorph, etc. via SOCKS proxy as Tor Pluggable Transports.

1.3. Misc.
(Online Gaming, File Transfer, VPN, etc.)
Some ISPs throttle P2P traffic as P2P traffic is mostly linked to transferring of large media files. Some countries either block VPN traffic or only allow some VPN services where the security keys are shared with the government authorities.

Solutions
OnionShare, Message Stream Encryption (MSE), etc. for file sharing. SoftEther uses https transport protocol for providing VPN service [112].

2. Types of Network Protocol Obfuscators
Obfuscators can be categorized in several types. There is no standard way of categorizing obfuscators. Some of the well-known types of obfuscators as described by Wang et al. [2] provide Randomizing, Protocol Mimicry, and Tunnelling. Most researchers and authors have their own categorisation and definition of which obfuscators should come under which category. For example, Khattak et al. [53] classify ScrambleSuit under protocol mimicry while Wang et al. [2] place ScrambleSuit with randomizers. However, in this paper, in most cases, categorization described by Wang et al. [2] is given a priority unless an evidence states otherwise.

2.1. Randomizers or Scramblers
A randomizer obfuscates traffic by making it look arbitrary [2]. This hides the "application-layer static fingerprints" of the traffic [2]. Randomizers are also sometimes referred to as scramblers [95].

Examples are Dust, obfs2/3/4, ScrambleSuit, and MSE [2, 62, 54].

2.2. Protocol Mimicry or Shape Shifters

A protocol mimicry system disguises traffic to look like traffic of a cover protocol [2]. Protocol Mimicry is also described as Shape Shifting [95]. In theory, it is probably the best form of protocol obfuscation. However, in practice it is not easy to implement perfect protocol mimicry [95]. The protocol mimicry client and server behave differently from real client and server, therefore, censors can always perform extra checks and determine that the traffic is not the real cover protocol but a fake or mimicked protocol [95].

Examples of protocol mimicry systems are Format Transforming Encryption (FTE), Marionette, CensorSpoofer, SkypeMorph, Dust2, MailMyWeb, TransTeg, and StegoTorus [2, 53, 95].

2.3. Tunnelling

According to Wang et al. [2], tunnelling mechanism involves sending data through a cover protocol which in a sense is just another form of mimicry. Tunnelling is also known as fronting [95].

An example of tunnelling technique is meek, Freewave, Facet, Castle, SWEET, JumpBox, and CloudTransport [2, 53, 54].

3. Traffic Morphing

Wright, C., Coulls, S., and Monrose, F. [9] introduced the idea of traffic morphing in 2009. The concept presented in the paper was to make "one class of traffic to look like another class" [9]. Wright, C., Coulls, S., and Monrose, F. proposed the use of convex optimisation for achieving utmost morphing [9].

Traffic morphing or traffic shaping is now a common topic whenever protocol obfuscation is discussed. However, there is no single term to describe traffic morphing and network protocol obfuscation. Protocol Masquerade can be a better term to describe both Protocol Obfuscation and Traffic Morphing as both are interdependent and can be unproductive without the presence of the other. Traffic morphing makes it harder to detect an obfuscated protocol.

4. Goals of Protocol Masquerade Process (GPMP)

The purpose of a network Protocol Masquerade process is to provide absolute unobservability. A successful Protocol Masquerade process achieves the following goals.

It **obfuscates** all the protocols in the network session.
- It makes sure that the number of protocols in the obfuscated network session is same as the number of protocols in the genuine network session.
- It applies the following on each protocol in the network session:
  - It makes the protocol look like a target protocol or it hides the protocol inside a target protocol so that the hidden or obfuscated protocol becomes undiscoverable between the sender and the final destination of the communication. This can be achieved by any of the three protocol obfuscation techniques randomizer, mimicry, or tunnelling.

And it **morphs** or shapes the traffic generated by protocol obfuscation.
- It gives traffic of the obfuscated protocol the same pattern and characteristics as the traffic of the cover protocol.
- Same rule applies to traffic of side protocols in the network session that often accompany the genuine protocol.
- The traffic morphing rule applies to traffic generated by any of the three protocol obfuscation techniques randomizer, mimicry, or tunnelling.

The concept of multiple protocols and side protocols within a session is taken from [3].

Success Criteria
A Protocol Masquerade system is considered successful when protocol obfuscation and traffic morphing has been applied on network traffic and the obfuscated protocol cannot be detected in the resulting traffic.

Similar (But Not So Similar) Work
Hjelmvik and John [12] defined two types of obfuscation, payload and flow-level. Although their work seems similar to the goals described above but the definitions have clear differences.

The definition of payload obfuscation described by Hjelmvik and John [12] is very similar to a randomizer and does not cover the other two protocol obfuscation techniques i.e. tunnelling and mimicry. Sometimes there are more than one protocol used in a genuine network session which is also not described in [12]. Hjelmvik and John suggested that encryption can be used to create payload obfuscation which is not the case anymore as encryption is widely used and censors are far too resourceful these days [12]. Research discussed throughout this paper suggests that it is possible to detect protocol obfuscation even when encryption is used. Similarly, the flow-level obfuscation described also suggests "randomizing" the packet flow features [12] which is not the same as traffic morphing described above. As described in the GPMP above, even when protocol randomizers obfuscate the traffic they should shape the traffic just like the target protocol. Therefore, the concept of randomizing traffic without making it morph traffic of a real protocol will do more harm than gain.

4. Systems, Tools, and Techniques in Detail

1. Tor

Tor is an overlay network consisting of nodes called relays [22]. Tor clients create a three-node encrypted connection through the Tor network [22]. Moghaddam described that Tor relays can be easily blocked because information about the relays is publicly available [8]. Hence, the Tor project implemented bridges which are not publicly listed making it harder for censors to find the bridges [8]. Tor facilitates in evading IP-based censorship filtering because of the vast number of proxies and Tor bridges that are in operation [2].

Similar to, uProxy and Lantern, Tor itself does not provide obfuscation. However, several systems in this study make use of Tor for the end-to-end implementation of protocol obfuscation of traffic. Therefore, the discussion of Tor directly and indirectly relates and impacts the study of some protocol obfuscation systems used with Tor as Pluggable Transport. And, so are the vulnerabilities and possible observability in Tor when used without a protocol obfuscation system, can impact the best possible results that can be achieved from a pluggable transport.

Tor has gained popularity since more and more countries are implementing state-wide internet censorship and monitoring systems. According to MIT News [68], Tor had 2.5 million daily users in 2015.

Tails, a Debian Linux distribution, aimed at providing anonymity as well as censorship circumvention utilises Tor for network connectivity [109, 110].

Tor is designed to support censorship circumvention and confidential internet use by providing anonymity [8]. Several email providers now also support Tor. ProtonMail provides end-to-end email encryption and it supports Tor network [67].

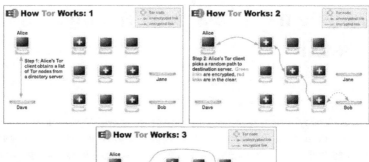

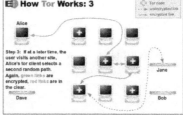

Figure 1: How Tor Works [113]

Attacks & Detection

Tor traffic can be identified when used without a pluggable transport (PT) [8, 65, 66].

Houmansadr et al. [65] noted that Tor relays can be easily blocked as the IP addresses of the relays are publicly listed and a similar observation was also made by Moghaddam [8].

McLachlan and Hopper [66] identified three faults in the bridge design; they are trivial to locate, they always accept a connection from Tor, and traffic in either direction between the bridge client disturbs the bridge operator traffic.

1.1. Pluggable Transports (PT)

Protocol obfuscation in Tor and similar network systems is evolving rapidly [93]. Pluggable Transports provide the ability to obfuscate network traffic. The shapeshifter project provides standards and means for building pluggable transports [90].

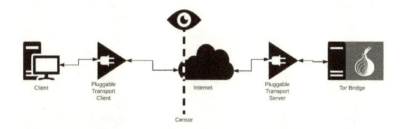

Figure 2: Tor Pluggable Transport (based on concept from [8])

Four pluggable transports are currently deployed by default with the Tor Browser [94]. The following table describes the list of pluggable transports for Tor taken from [94, 95, 96, 97, 98]. And status of the project is described as stalled if no update to the code appeared in the last two year.

PT	Works With	Working Versions Available	Deployed with Tor Browser	Status	Being Developed
obfs4	Tor	√	√	Available	
meek	Psiphon, Tor	√	√	Available	
FTE	Tor, Lanter, uProxy	√	√	Available	
ScrambleSuit	Tor	√	√	Available	
Dust	Tor	√		Deprecated	
StegoTorus	Tor	√		Deprecated	
obfs3	Tor, Lantern	√		Deprecated	
obfs2	Tor	√		Deprecated	
Flashproxy	Tor	√		Deprecated	

- 23 -

SnowFlake	Tor			Alpha available	√
basket2	Tor			Code available	√
SkypeMorph*	Tor			Project stalled	
bananaphone	Tor			Project Stalled	√
LODP	Tor			Project stalled	
sshproxy	Tor			Project stalled	√
hexchat	Tor			Project stalled	√
Dust2	Tor			Project stalled	√
Code Talker Tunnel*	Tor			Project stalled	
obfuscatedssh	Psiphon			Unknown	
Socks-rtc	uProxy			Unknown	
flashlight	Lantern			Unknown	

*SkypeMorph and Code Talker Tunnel are similar projects.

Table 1: Status of Pluggable Transports

1.2. Communication over Tor

Tor can be used for almost any communication over the internet and not just for browsing. Any software that supports internet connections via a SOCKS proxy can be used for connecting to Tor and if a pluggable transport is deployed and configured then the connection will automatically go via the PT and receive obfuscation from the PT.

1.2.1. File Share

OnionShare, a purposely built system for Tor, can be used for sharing files. Most of the file sharing software support connections via SOCKS like µTorrent, BitTorrent, and Vuze. These software can be configure to connect to Tor via SOCKS proxy.

1.2.2. Email Client

Any email client that supports SOCKS proxy can be used for connecting to Tor. For example, Thunderbird with TorBirdy installed will route the traffic via Tor daemon service [100]. If there is a Pluggable Transport PT is deployed, Tor daemon service will route the traffic via the PT.

1.2.3. Email Server

OnionMail [101] is an out-of-the-box mail server built to run on Tor and it claims to provide anonymity and has the capability to talk to the Internet outside the Tor network.

2. BitTorrent's MSE

MSE or Message Stream Encryption is an application layer obfuscated protocol [12] designed to provide obfuscation for the BitTorrent protocol [62].

Obfuscation Type	Randomizer [62].
Claims	"To provide a completely random-looking header and (optionally) payload to avoid passive protocol identification and traffic shaping" [62].
External Confirmation	MSE is an old system. From the beginning critics were sceptical about the success of MSE. When MSE was just seven years old Brooks and Aslanian called it a "wasteful of resources and does not provide the type of protection that the authors desired" [81]. There has always been a misunderstanding about what MSE is supposed to achieve, security or protocol misidentification. Cohen, inventor of BitTorrent, said MSE "temporarily evades traffic shaping" and it does not provide anonymity [82].
Implementation	"The 2 different payload encryption methods plaintext transmission and RC4 provide a different degree of protocol obfuscation, security and speed. Where the

	plaintext mode only provides basic anti-shaping obscurity, no security and low CPU usage the RC4 encryption obfuscates the entire stream and not only the header and adds some cryptographic security at the price of spent CPU cycles." [62]
Has this system been attacked?	Yes [12].
Is MSE generated traffic detectable?	Yes [12]. MSE "can be identified by fingerprinting statistically measurable properties of TCP and UDP sessions" [12].

Does MSE offer confidentiality and censorship circumvention?	
Internet Browsing	No.
Email	No.
Misc. (gaming, file sharing, etc.)	No.

Attacks & Detection

Hjelmvik and John [12] explained that the BitTorrent applications Vuze and µTorrent do not implement full randomness according to the MSE specification. They added that for reducing traffic overhead only half the padding was used which makes these applications detectable by Statistical Protocol Identification (SPID) algorithm [12]. Zink and Waldvogel [63] also confirmed that they did not find any BitTorrent client that correctly implemented the MSE standard.

Even if the full randomness of 512 bytes is used, Hjelmvik and John [12] suggest that flow-level analysis can be effectively used to detect the MSE traffic.

Furthermore, Hjelmvik and John [12] observed that MSE uses Diffie-Hellman (D-H) key exchange which makes the protocol effortlessly recognisable.

3. Obfs4

Obfs3 could be detected by active probing and also did not hide flow signature [1]. Its successor obfs4 resembles ScrambleSuit in many ways [61], "but has a different public key obfuscation technique and a protocol for one-way authentication. The project is written in Go and it is faster than ScrambleSuit." [104]

Obfuscation Type	Randomizer [104, 54]. The author [61] of obfs4 explained that it is similar to ScrambleSuit.
Claims	Delivers data integrity and authentication while providing protocol obfuscation based on SSH or TLS [111].
External Confirmation	Obfs4 circumvents censors and its traffic goes through DPIs undetected by applying content randomization along with implementation of variable packet sizes and randomizing inter-arrival times of packets [54].
Implementation	The handshake involves full key exchange [61]. Backward compatible to obfs3 and obfs2 [61].
Has this system been attacked?	Yes [2].
Is obfs4 generated traffic detectable?	Yes [2].

Does obfs4 offer confidentiality and censorship circumvention?	
Internet Browsing	Yes. Obfs4 is a Tor pluggable transport.
Email	Yes, for SOCKS compatible email clients. See §1.2.2.
Misc. (gaming, file sharing, etc.)	Yes, for SOCKS compatible clients. See §1.2.1.

Attacks & Detection

obfs4 shipped with vanilla Tor is blocked in Kazakhstan since second half of 2016 [99].

Wang et al. claimed successfully discovering traffic generated by obfs4 (or its predecessor obfs3) with 100% accuracy by observing the first packet (with a 0.2% false-positive rate) [2]. They noted that all content in the first message of obfs4 is encrypted contrary to traffic of genuine SSH and TLS protocols which have plaintext header [2]. Furthermore, Wang et al. performed several entropy-based tests to perfectly discover obfs4 on a real network traffic (with a low false-positive rate) [2].

4. Flash Proxies

Fifield et al. [22] suggested a system for creating a large number of short-lived browser-based proxies called flash proxies.

When observing the flash proxies web page, it becomes evident that the number of users has never been high enough, that the authors hoped for in the paper, for censor circumvention to work effectively [35]. It is possible that the Flash Proxy authors are trying to keep a low profile for their system and do not wish to draw attention. As recently as June 2014, Tor Project webpages show that interest in Flash Proxies was still thriving [87, 88]. Therefore, the real number of users remains unknown though not as high as the authors needed for the system to work effectively.

Feamster et al. [84] presented a similar system, Infranet, back in 2002 which also relied on a large number of web servers to act as proxies.

Figure 3: Flash Proxy browser plugin [103]. Visiting a flash proxy enabler page and leaving it open helps others circumvent censorship.

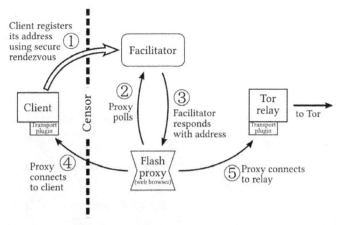

Figure 4: Flash Proxies Architecture [22]

Obfuscation Type	Tunnelling.
Claims	It is difficult for censors to block a very large number of IP addresses if used as proxies [22]. Field testing done by Fifield et al. [22] in December 2011 showed that flash proxies worked in China.
External Confirmation	FlashProxy is another way of bypassing censors [104].
Implementation	Flash proxies require a large number of people visit a webpage and leave the webpage open in their browser (assuming that they are online all this time when someone is connected to the proxy) [22]. "It is a proxy that runs in a web browser and checks for clients that request access, then it transmits data between those clients and the TOR relay. The technologies used in implementing Flashproxy are JavaScript and WebSocket, and the objective of this project is to outrun the censors' ability to recognize the bridge's IP address, by creating many temporary bridge IP addresses." [104]

Has this system been attacked?	Yes [53].
Is Flash Proxies generated traffic detectable?	Yes [53].

Does FlashProxy offer confidentiality and censorship circumvention?	
Internet Browsing	Yes [22].
Email	Yes, via any email client that supports connections via SOCKS proxy. See 1.2.2.
Misc. (gaming, file sharing, etc.)	Yes, via any client that supports connections via SOCKS proxy. See 1.2.1.

(Flash Proxy project has recently been deprecated, according to their website, and the website now advises users to use SnowFlake which is a Tor pluggable transport built using similar technique [35].)

Attacks & Detection

Flash Proxies do not perform content and flow obfuscation, and also do not make the user anonymous [53] which makes them very easily detectable and not fit-for-purpose from the end-to-end obfuscation point of view.

Some attacks discussed in the paper by Fifield et al. [22]:

- Client enumeration: Censor queries the facilitator and gets a list of IP addresses of circumventors.
- Flooding client registrations: In this attack an adversary sends too many fake client IP addresses to the facilitator. Fifield et al. do not see this as a viable attack and propose some mitigations but even the mitigations will not stop a state-run censor to carry out such an attack on the flash proxies. For example, one suggested mitigation is not to accept too many registrations from an IP address. State-run censors like GFW has too many IP addresses at its disposal. GFW can flood registrations originating from thousands of IP addresses making the mitigation ineffective. Another proposed mitigation is to

have many free proxies. Again, a state-run censor can easily create enough fake clients to keep the available proxies busy.
- Protocol fingerprinting: Flash proxy traffic can be separated from regular TCP connections.

Attacks not mentioned in the paper by Fifield et al. [22]:
- If the censor detects, by any means, that an IP address has requested a facilitator for flash proxy registration; all the censor has to do is to act as a proxy and establish an outgoing connection to the client. This will confirm to the censor whether an IP address is seeking a flash proxy connection or not. A similar attack by the GFW is observed by Winter and Crandall [30] in which GFW creates a Tor connection to harvest and blacklist Tor bridges.
- In December 2011, Fifield et al. [22] successfully used flash proxies from China. Most likely, the test passed because the number of connections to the flash proxies was not high enough to raise suspicion for the GFW to react to it. A probe from GFW would have been eminent if the number of connections had significantly increased.

Some of the other issues apparent with flash proxy architecture are:
- The facilitator keeps note of proxy and client pairs. In a real world implementation, a vast number of facilitators will be required. How the proxy and client pair information flows between the different facilitators is not discussed in the paper by Fifield et al. [22].
- It is understood that all facilitators will be blocked by the censors. However, it is not clear how the clients are sending data to the facilitator.
- By some means the facilitator endpoint will be required to have a large number of IP addresses. Otherwise, censors will blacklist the facilitator's IP address. This is not discussed in the paper by Fifield et al. [22] either.
- It was assumed by Fifield et al. [22] that most proxies will be idle most of the time. However, the reason for such an assumption was not clear in the paper.
- Study carried out by Wang et al. [2], obfuscation can be detected with high accuracy because of its pattern and behaviour. However, how flash proxies handle this issue was not discussed in-depth by Fifield et al. [22]. In real world scenario, if flash proxies are used at a very large scale, it is safe to assume that there will be many broken connections between the clients and inactive/closed proxies. This would create an observable pattern.

- Another observable pattern is that the client will receive a connection from an IP address i.e. a proxy even when the client never sent a GET request to the that IP address.
- What if the client is using the internet for illegal purposes e.g. a drug trade? In such a case, an ordinary citizen, whose browser was used for providing the proxy, will get into trouble with the law. Will an ordinary citizen knowingly take such a risk?
- Not sure how a flash proxy will work in a corporate network? Some corporate networks, e.g. banks, have their own digital certificates created from their own certificate authority. All browsers used on the machines on such a corporate network have these digital certificates installed. There are servers deployed specifically for the purpose of monitoring data that goes in or out of the network by decrypting everything that is passing through the network. How an encrypted Tor data can pass through such a network without raising alarms?

5. eMule Protocol Obfuscation

eMule is a P2P file sharing software. eMule is a client for eDonkey [12]. Obfuscation protocol used in eMule is called EncryptedStreamSocket [12].

Obfuscation Type	Randomizer.
Claims	Avoidance of throttling of file sharing traffic by the internet service providers [11].
External Confirmation	In 2009, Freire, Carvalho, and Pereira [105] presented at a conference the issues of identifying and stopping eMule generated traffic; calling it "one of the most difficult to detect among popular peer-to-peer file sharing applications".
Implementation	Random data stream [11].
Has this system been attacked?	Yes [12].
Is eMule generated traffic detectable?	Yes [11, 12, 105]. According the eMule wiki the obfuscation is detectable and does not implement confidential file sharing [11].

Does FreeWave offer confidentiality and censorship circumvention?	
File Sharing	No [11].

Attacks & Detection

Freire, Carvalho, and Pereira [105] detected eMule traffic from its signature using snort rules (see appendix B2 and B3) even when eMule was configured to use maximum obfuscation. They also wrote some snort rules to detect BitTorrent traffic and were surprised to find out that snort rules for BitTorrent were detecting eMule obfuscated traffic [105].

Hjelmvik and John [12] observed that eMule protocol obfuscation for TCP always behaved in a similar fashion. They noted that first four packets of every session had the same signature [12]:

  Packet 1. Client→Server: 12 to 267 bytes
  Packet 2. Server→Client: 6 to 261 bytes
  Packet 3. Client→Server: 98 to 113 bytes
  Packet 4. Server→Client: 103 to 358 bytes

They also noted that the first 20 packets served between client and server had nearly 5 packets of size 9 to 11 bytes and nearly 5 packets of size 54 to 59 bytes [12]. Packet sizes were maximum segment size after the encryption handshake [12]. Hjelmvik and John observed that the best way to detect eDonkey TCP protocol obfuscation is by flow analysis [12].

6. FreeWave

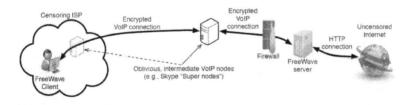

Figure 5: FreeWave Architecture [65]

Obfuscation Type	Possible Protocol Mimicry. Though described as Tunnelling by [54]. (Wang et al. [2] noted that tunnelling is just another form of protocol mimicry.)
Claims	Easily deployable censorship resisting system utilizing VOIP connection via Skype super nodes for achieving unobservability [65].
External Confirmation	FreeWave, though very much alike with SkypeMorph, is more advanced as it drives VoIP traffic through a virtual modem [106].
Implementation	FreeWave transfers data over VoIP connections via the FreeWave server that has two roles; it un-obfuscates the traffic and behaves as a proxy by routing the traffic to its destination [65].
Has this system been attacked?	Yes [106].
Is FreeWave generated traffic detectable?	Yes [106].

Does FreeWave offer confidentiality and censorship circumvention?	
Internet Browsing	Yes [65].
Email	Yes [65].
Misc. (gaming, file sharing, etc.)	Yes [65].

Attacks & Detection

Content mismatch occurs when the content that was expected and the obfuscated content added to the cover protocol differ from each other [106]. FreeWave is a perfect example where a content mismatch occurs even though the cover protocol is faultlessly matched [106]. Geddes, Schuchard, and Hopper stated that FreeWave modem has audio signal significantly different from real human speech audio signals [106], therefore, they concluded that a spoken language has length sequence much higher in variance than FreeWave running over Skype. Li, Schliep, and Hopper also observed that dropping 90% of packets in less than a second can completely disrupt FreeWave communication [60].

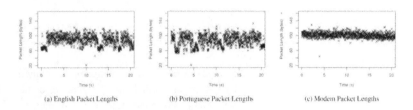

(a) English Packet Lengths (b) Portuguese Packet Lengths (c) Modem Packet Lengths

Figure 6: Packet length of English and Portuguese speech over Skype vs. modem audio sent over Skype [106]

7. SkypeMorph

Moghaddam developed a system for obfuscating Tor traffic in a Skype video call while also morphing the target protocol's traffic [8]. It was noted that it is also possible to adapt the system for other UDP-based protocols [8].

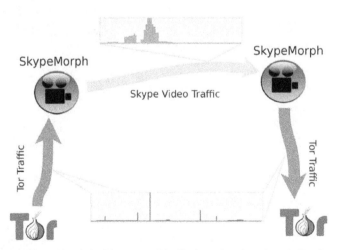

Figure 7: SkypeMorph Architecture – Distribution of packet sizes in Tor (bottom) vs Skype Video (top) is displayed in the histograms [8]

Obfuscation Type	Protocol Mimicry [3, 54].
Claims	SkypeMorph provides the critically required obfuscation client and the Tor bridge to circumvent deep packet inspection [8]. SkypeMorph makes it harder for censor to detect its traffic by generating output that is looks like an ordinary Skype video call [8]. Moghaddam argues that traffic morphing is often overlooked by researchers and SkypeMorph offers better traffic morphing than just a "naïve traffic shaping" method [8].
External Confirmation	SkypeMorph is one of the most famous Tor pluggable transport systems in terms of coverage in the research papers. However, the fame came at a price. SkypeMorph is also one of the most criticized obfuscation systems. No independent external confirmation was found in favour of SkypeMorph. SkypeMorph definitely took the fight to a different level by incorporating protocol obfuscation and traffic morphing into a single system i.e. by trying to create a perfect protocol masquerade system.
Implementation	Hides bridge and client traffic in Skype video call [8]. Pluggable transport for Tor [8].
Has this system been attacked?	Yes [3].
Is SkypeMorph generated traffic detectable?	Yes [3].

Does SkypeMorph offer confidentiality and censorship circumvention?	
Internet Browsing	Yes [8].
Email	Yes. Any email client that uses SOCKS can utilise SkyeMorph possibly because it uses SOCKS proxy; however not mentioned in the documentation in [8].

Misc. (gaming, file sharing, etc.)	Yes. Any software application that uses SOCKS can utilise SkyeMorph possibly because it uses SOCKS proxy; however not mentioned in the documentation in [8].

Attacks & Detection

Houmansadr, Brubaker, and Shmatikov [3] observed that although SkypeMorph mimics Skype protocol by creating datagrams matching distributions of a Skype video chat but SkypeMorph implementation fails to imitate TCP control channel that is present in a real Skype session. Furthermore, they validated that SkypeMorph does not provide unobservability because its traffic is different from real Skype traffic and can be detected by passive attacks [3]. They used two classes of passive attacks; one for detecting partial replications and second class manipulated the known behaviour of SkypeMorph that it uses pre-recorded real Skype traffic patterns for shaping the obfuscated protocol traffic [3]. Houmansadr, Brubaker, and Shmatikov concluded that SkypeMorph does not stand a chance even against a very basic censor [3].

Attack	Imitation Requirement*	Adversary**	Result
Skype HTTP update traffic	SideProtocols	LO/OB/OM	Satisfied
Skype login traffic	SideProtocols	LO/OB/OM	Satisfied
SoM (start of message) field of Skype UDP packets	Content	LO/OB/OM	Failed
Traffic statistics	Pattern	LO/OM	Satisfied
Periodic message exchanges	SideProtocols	LO/OB/OM	Failed
Typical Skype client behaviour	IntraDepend	LO/OM	Failed
TCP control channel	SideProtocols	LO/OB/OM	Failed

* SideProtocols = protocols that run side-by-side to the main session, IntraDepend = Several simultaneous connections interdependent on each other for a single protocol session
** LO = Local adversary, OB = State-level oblivious adversary, OM = State-level omniscient adversary
Figure 8: Passive Attacks for Detecting SkypeMorph (taken from [3])

Houmansadr, Riedl, Borisov, and Singer [65] observed that server obfuscation is implemented in SkpeMorph design which makes the Tor bridge vulnerable to detection and blacklisting by the censors.

Geddes et al. [106] established that voice and video protocols are not good cover protocols when it comes to protocol obfuscation. They noted that these cover protocols are peer-to-peer and are loss-tolerant while the SkypeMorph obfuscated traffic is loss-intolerant [106]. They proved that it is possible for a censor to block SkypeMorph traffic, without affecting a real Skype traffic, by attacking how SkypeMorph ACK packet management is implemented [106].

Li, Schliep, and Hopper [60] also found flaws in SkypeMorph. They noticed that SkypeMorph does not imitate the way real Skype system handles "network conditions" [60]. SkypeMorph does not properly mimic Skype UDP packets for missing SoM field [60]. Li, Schliep, and Hopper also observed that dropping 5% of packets in less than a second can completely disrupt SkypeMorph communication [60].

8. FTE

In a paper [10] by Dyer et al., a new cryptographic primitive called Format-Transforming Encryption (FTE) was introduced. They devised a very lightweight method for mimicking protocols as it has no latency cost and only 16% bandwidth overhead in comparison with SSH tunnels [10]. Their proposed method can be used to convert symmetric encryption ciphertext into any desired format [10]. They observed that many enterprise level DPI systems use regular expression to determine if packet contents match fingerprint of a protocol [10]. They created a tool which takes regular expression of the fingerprint of a protocol as an input and then creates ciphertexts that match the regex or in other words match the fingerprint of the target protocol [10]. This facilitated them to successfully trick regular expression based DPI systems in misclassifying protocols [10]. During testing of FTE client on a server located in China, Dyer's team noted that websites that were otherwise blocked by the Great Firewall were accessible via FTE [10]. They also observed that Tor which is ordinarily blocked in China worked when used with a FTE proxy [10].

The following table covers Format Transforming Encryption – FTE implementation for Tor and uProxy.

Obfuscation Type	Protocol Mimicry [2].
Claims	Dyer et al. [10] claim the following: • FTE encrypts application layer communication for achieving misidentification by the DPI systems. • DPI systems used were at enterprise standard. Dyer et al. asserted that incorporating FTE proxy with Tor provides censor evasion. They tested FTE proxy in the domain of Great Firewall to prove their theory. • FTE proxy has no effect on latency. • FTE proxy creates only 16% of extra bandwidth expense. • FTE is a better choice compared to obfsproxy. Obfsproxy uses D-H key exchange which provides random fingerprint however, it does not provide protocol misclassification.
External Confirmation	Provides efficient and "light-weight mimicry" compared to other obfuscators [2].
Implementation	Implemented as a pluggable transport for Tor and is also used by uProxy [2].
Has this system been attacked?	Yes [2].
Is FTE generated traffic detectable?	Yes [2].

Does FTE offer confidentiality and censorship circumvention?	
Internet Browsing	Yes [10].
Email	Yes, via any email client that supports connections via SOCKS proxy. See 1.2.2.
Misc. (gaming, file sharing, etc.)	Yes, via any client that supports connections via SOCKS proxy. See 1.2.1.

Attacks & Detection

Dyer, Coull, and Shrimpton [54] noted that programmable obfuscation systems merge mimicry and randomization. They also observed that FTE is fast and can mimic an extensive number of protocols but the true strength of FTE lies in obfuscating the application layer content. FTE does not implement "statistical properties, protocol semantics, or other potentially distinguishing traffic features" [54].

Jones et al. [52] observed that FTE can generate "non-compliant packets", however, they did not provide solid evidence or backup their claim with further information.

Wang et al. [2] observed that content length attack does not provide the success rate they were trying to achieve. They recognised that inaccuracy of message content length can be caused by several reasons including early connection termination, transfer of encoding fields, extra control bytes in the message body appended by some internet browsers, bugs in the browser code, and non-ASCII characters in the content [2].

Wang et al. [2] noted that FTE traffic can be discovered by "tests on the entropy and length of the URI appearing in the first FTE-produced packet". They observed that the first message is a HTTP GET request with URI with large Shannon entropies [2]. The explanation provided by Wang et al. for this behaviour is the encoding of ciphertexts from bits to bytes [2]. They added that it is trivial to conclude that the protocol obfuscation system used is FTE if the URI from the initial HTTP flow GET request contains entropy of minimum 5.5 bits [2]. To get a better detection of FTP data, they noted that URIs in FTE's HTTP requests always had a length of 239 bytes [2]. This improved their false-positive rates to only 264 for ten million samples tested which were based on from office, cloud and wifi datasets [2].

9. ScrambleSuit

ScrambleSuit is a transport protocol designed to survive active probing and it avoids creation of a flow signature or recognisable repeating pattern [1]. According to the makers of ScrambleSuit, it implements a lean obfuscation layer on top of TCP and by design ScrambleSuit provides pseudo-random payload, its polymorphic, makes use of shared secret, and has a moderate protocol overhead [1].

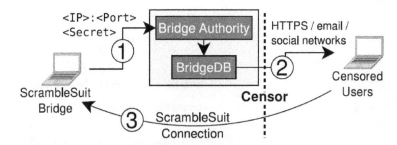

ScrambleSuit bridges send their descriptor to the Tor project's bridge authority ①. From there, it is distributed to censored users who learn about IP address, port and the secret out-of-band ②. Finally, direct connections can be established ③.

Figure 9: ScrambleSuit Connection Sequence (copied from [1])

Obfuscation Type	Randomizer [1, 54].
Claims	Survives active probing, does not create a recognisable repeating pattern, and implements a two-way authentication mechanism [1].
External Confirmation	"The exchanged traffic between the TOR client and the TOR bridge is encrypted, authenticated and disguised. From a technical point of view, this protocol protects against active probing attacks and can generate unique flow signature by altering the inter-arrival time and the packet length distribution. As an observation, ScrambleSuit can transport many other protocols besides TOR, like VPN, SSH etc." [104]
Implementation	Obfuscation layer on top of TCP [1]. ScrambleSuit requires an application to support SOCKS [1].
Has this system been attacked?	Yes [85].

Is ScrambleSuit generated traffic detectable?	Yes [85].

Does ScrambleSuit offer confidentiality and censorship circumvention?	
Internet Browsing	Yes [1].
Email	Yes, for SOCKS compatible email clients. See §1.2.2.
Misc. (gaming, file sharing, etc.)	Yes, for SOCKS compatible clients. See §1.2.1.

Attacks & Detection

ScrambleSuit is a randomizer and randomizers have been successfully attacked and detected by Wang et al. in [2]. However, no detailed research was found to indicate that ScrambleSuit has been successfully attacked and detected except for the following two which do not provide in depth details of the threat models.

Khattak et al. observed that ScrambleSuit does not provide user and publisher anonymity [53] while Khattak, Simon, and Murdoch [85] noted that ScrambleSuit is quite resilient to attacks, however, the IP addresses of its proxies are common knowledge which makes it vulnerable to censors.

10. Meek

Meek uses domain fronting [49] for achieving obfuscation.

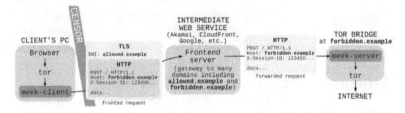

Figure 10: How meek works? [49]

Obfuscation Type	Tunnelling [2].
Claims	Meek provides obfuscation that is built for censorship circumvention [49].
External Confirmation	Wang et al. [2] called Meek "a state-of-the-art tunneling obfuscator".
Implementation	Meek is a Pluggable transport for Tor that uses domain fronting, for sending messages to Tor relays, by utilising different domain names at different communication layers [49]. It appears to be communicating with a non-tor address while in reality it is communicating with a Tor relay [49].
Has this system been attacked?	Yes [2].
Is Meek generated traffic detectable?	Yes [2].

Does meek offer confidentiality and censorship circumvention?	
Internet Browsing	Yes [49].
Email	Yes, for SOCKS compatible email clients. See §1.2.2.
Misc. (gaming, file sharing, etc.)	Yes, for SOCKS compatible clients. See §1.2.1.

Attacks & Detection

Since May 2016, meek-google does not work anymore [64]. According to Fifield, D. the reason meek-google stopped working was purely because of Google terminating the reflector web application in their Cloud Platform and had nothing to do with censors [64]. However, meek-amazon and meek-azure are still in operation [49].

Wang et al. [2] believed that meek generated traffic is the most difficult to detect and classify using a deep packet inspection mechanism. They observed that using non-machine learning entropy based attacks was not successful against meek [2]. Instead Wang et al. detected meek generated traffic by using machine learning.

They learnt that classifiers that are trained by exercising "traffic-analysis-type techniques" successfully spot meek obfuscation [2]. Wang et al. observed that although machine learning based attacks are more successful however, they were less efficient in performance compared to other attacks [2].

Meek shipped with vanilla Tor browser bundle is blocked in Kazakhstan since second half of 2016 [99].

11. StegoTorus

StegoTorus hides tor traffic in commonly used cover channels like HTML, Flash SWF, and PDF [4]. StegoTorus is a Tor pluggable transport which extends SOCKS [4, 6]. StegoTorus can be utilised by any application that uses SOCKS [4]. StegoTorus client chops traffic into data blocks, encrypts the data blocks, performs protocol mimicry on the blocks, delivers them in random order over several connections to the StegoTorus server, and the server reassembles and unencrypts the blocks before passing them on to relay network [4].

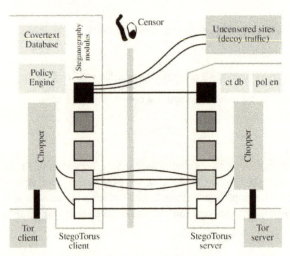

Figure 11: StegoTorus Architecture [4]

StegoTorus architecture is quite simple. It chops a message into parts, applies steganography, sends it over the wire in multiple streams, performs reverse steganography, and puts the parts together to build the whole message [4]. The output of steganography in StegoTorus creates arbitrary sized blocks for achieving randomness [4].

Obfuscation Type	Protocol Mimicry [2, 54]. Randomizer [4].
Claims	Hides traffic in harmless protocols like unencrypted HTTP [4]. Tough against fingerprinting attacks [4].
External Confirmation	Back in 2012, when pluggable transports were relatively new, StegoTorus was considered better than obfs2 because it was considered more difficult to block; it was more resilient to passive attacks [102].
Implementation	Pluggable transport for Tor [4]. Mimics HTTP, Skype, and Ventrilo protocols [3]. Embedded stenography [3, 4].
Has this system been attacked?	Yes [3].
Is StegoTorus generated traffic detectable?	Yes [3].

Does StegoTorus offer confidentiality and censorship circumvention?	
Internet Browsing	Yes [4].
Email	Yes, for SOCKS compatible email clients [4]. See §1.2.2.
Misc. (gaming, file sharing, etc.)	Yes, for SOCKS compatible clients [4]. See §1.2.1.

Attacks & Detection

Dyer, Coull, and Shrimpton [54] observed that protocol obfuscation systems that utilise mimicry techniques usually implement a light version of the mimicry of statistical properties of a network connection. StegoTorus limits itself by using an already saved collection of HTTP messages for performing mimicry which restricts it to the statistical properties of the previously saved collection of HTTP messages [54].

Houmansadr, Brubaker, and Shmatikov [3] observed that although StegoTorus mimics Skype protocol by creating datagrams matching distributions of a Skype video chat but its implementation fails to imitate TCP control channel that is present in a real Skype session. Furthermore, just like SkypeMorph, Houmansadr, Brubaker, and Shmatikov proved that StegoTorus also does not provide unobservability because its traffic is different from real Skype traffic and can be detected by a passive attack [3].

Attack	Imitation Requirement	Adversary*	Result
Skype HTTP update traffic	SideProtocols	LO/OB/OM	Failed
Skype login traffic	SideProtocols	LO/OB/OM	Failed
SoM (start of message) field of Skype UDP packets	Content	LO/OB/OM	Failed
Traffic statistics	Pattern	LO/OM	Satisfied
Periodic message exchanges	SideProtocols	LO/OB/OM	Failed
Typical Skype client behaviour	IntraDepend	LO/OM	Failed
TCP control channel	SideProtocols	LO/OB/OM	Failed

* SideProtocols = protocols that run side-by-side to the main session, IntraDepend = Several simultaneous connections interdependent on each other for a single protocol session
** LO = Local adversary, OB = State-level oblivious adversary, OM = State-level omniscient adversary
Table 2: Passive Attacks for Detecting SkypeMorph (taken from [3])

Houmansadr, Brubaker, and Shmatikov concluded that just like SkypeMorph StegoTorus is not effective even against an incredibly basic censor [3].

Weinber et al., also discussed that it is possible, though costly, to detect the "simple schemes" of the steganography design proposed in their original paper [4].

Moghaddam noted that a censor can identify abnormal web traffic created by StegoTorus [8].

Murdoch and Kadianakis [102] argued that StegoTorus was more resistant to blocking but observed that StegoTorus chopper was more complex therefore was less efficient. They also noted that improvements could be made in better obscuring of Tor's unique packet size [102]. Murdoch and Kadianakis also suggested that high entropy packets could expose StegoTorus generated traffic [102].

12. Dust

From grounds-up, Dust (version 1) was built to follow Köpsell's principle of "blocking-resistance as a necessary prerequisite to achieve censorship resistance" [50].

Obfuscation Type	Randomizer [2, 62, 54].
Claims	Brandon [50] designed the Dust protocol to bypass DPIs which use fingerprinting for detecting protocols. All Dust packets look similar because they are made of "encrypted or random single-use bytes" [50]. Implements Köpsell's model for handshake [50].
External Confirmation	Murdoch and Kadianakis observed that Dust is built with tough threat model in mind and it allows padding to hide actual packet length [102].
Implementation	Communication resembles random data and uses padding to hide packet length [1].
Has this system been attacked?	Yes, theoretically [1].
Is Dust generated traffic detectable?	Yes, by inference [1].

| "Key exchange is handled out-of-band" and Dust does not change "flow signature" [1]. | |

Does Dust offer confidentiality and censorship circumvention?	
Internet Browsing	Yes* [50].
Email	Theoretically Dust has the capability but no solution was found that offered email capability by implementing Dust.
Misc. (gaming, file sharing, etc.)	Same as above.

* Though there are some limitation as mentioned by Brandon [50] in the design paper, one of which is the lack of disguise for sender and recipient IP addresses and ports. Dust relies on other tools to provide the full end-to-end censorship circumvention [50].

Attacks & Detection
Murdoch and Kadianakis noted that packets generated by Dust stick out [102].

Winter, Pulls, and Fuss [1] observed that traffic generated by Dust looks like random data, however, one of the issues is out of band key exchange. They further added that although Dust hides the real packet length with padding but cannot modify its flow signature [1]. This is a very important observation because DPI systems can easily identify Dust just because of the flow signature.

13. Infranet

Infranet obfuscation system was designed by Feamster et al. [84] back in 2002 which shows that the idea of censorship circumvention is as old as the censors themselves. Infranet design implements unobservability by hiding data communication between the Infranet "requester" and "responder" over a stealthy communication tunnel [84]. System relies on web server known as responders that are not blocked to pass the request to the blocked web servers. A similar system was designed by Jones et al. [52] called Facade which also uses covert communication in HTTP.

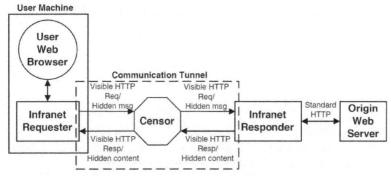

Figure 12: Infranet architecture [84]

Obfuscation Type	Tunnelling [84]. Mimicry [8].
Claims	"A system that enables clients to surreptitiously retrieve sensitive content via cooperating Web servers distributed across the global Internet" [84]. "Infranet can successfully circumvent several sophisticated censoring techniques, ranging from active attacks to passive attacks to impersonation" [84].
External Confirmation	Infranet offers superior deniability than Facade [52]. Infranet hides requests in HTTP protocol messages for achieving unobservability [8].
Implementation	"Infranet uses a tunnel protocol that provides a covert communication channel between its clients and servers, modulated over standard HTTP transactions that resemble innocuous Web browsing" [84].
Has this system been attacked?	Yes [8].
Is Infranet generated traffic detectable?	Yes [8].

Does Infranet offer confidentiality and censorship circumvention?	
Internet Browsing	Yes [84].
Email	No.
Misc. (online gaming, VPNs, etc.)	No.

Attacks & Detection

Infranet depends on a large number of unblocked web server to act as responders. This idea is also suggested in the design of Flash Proxies [22].

There are some assumptions made in the design. For example, guessing that if an Infranet responder is detected by a censor, the censor will be hesitant to block all communication to and from the responder which also includes the regular web content offered by the responder. It is evident that these days censors have become very aggressive and there is no reason for censors not to block all traffic to and from such a web server.

Distribution of addresses of the responder is also a big challenge. It is easier to give addresses to a small group of trusted users but difficult to implement such a solution on a large scale as adversaries can also get hold of the address and simply block them. The solution suggested for this problem is to allow users in the future to download the software directly from the responders. It is also clear how it will be successful in practice.

Infranet is a well thought through system for its time. However, now the state-run censors are very powerful and sophisticated. A simple threat model where the attacker is monitoring abnormal web traffic can identify and block Ifranet as observed by Moghaddam therefore, the system does not offer enough deniability necessary for successful censorship circumvention [8]. Similarly, Weinberg et al. noted a limitation in Infranet that it lacks "anonymity guarantees" that is provided by Tor [4].

14. CensorSpoofer

CensorSpoofer mimics VoIP traffic and is a standalone system [3]. CensorSpoofer assumes that all users are adversaries therefore it does not expose address of proxies to genuine users [108]. Geddes, Schuchard, and Hopper noted that CensorSpoofer uses mimicry and utilises VoIP protocol over SIP for downstream [106].

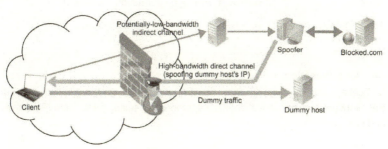

Figure 13: The CensorSpoofer framework [108]

Obfuscation Type	Protocol Mimicry [3, 106]. Tunnelling [54].
Claims	Wang et al. [108] proposed CensorSpoofer for mitigating the insider attack where a censor fakes as a legitimate user.
External Confirmation	No external source found that attacked the system and confirmed the claims of the authors of CensorSpoofer.
Implementation	Separate channels for upstream and downstream; steganography implemented in the low bandwidth upstream channel while IP spoofing used in high bandwidth downstream [1].
Has this system been attacked?	Yes [3, 106].

Is CensorSpoofer generated traffic detectable?	Yes [3].

Does CensorSpoofer offer confidentiality and censorship circumvention?	
Internet Browsing	Yes [108].
Email	Unsure as not enough information was found.
Misc. (gaming, file sharing, etc.)	Unsure as not enough information was found.

Attacks & Detection

Li, Schliep, and Hopper [60] argue that CensorSpoofer does not imitate the real SIP client properly because it does not appropriately select the spoofed IP address and port.

Houmansadr et al. observed that CensorSpoofer requires disclosure of secret with its clients which creates a question of scalability [65].

Houmansadr, Brubaker, and Shmatikov noted that CensorSpoofer prototype impersonates Ekiga, a SIP client [3]. It replaces the messages in the tags of the SIP header with a hash of spoofed IP address [3]. Similar to a real SIP client, CensorSpoofer client closes the connection if a censor changes the spoofed address [3]. However, Houmansadr, Brubaker and Shmatikov proposed a rather inexpensive attacked by a censor, unlike a genuine SIP client, the CensorSpoofer client will close a connection if the censor replaces the hash value in header tag to a different value [3].

Furthermore, Houmansadr, Brubaker, and Shmatikov [3] also observed that a censor can probe an IP address to verify if it running a legitimate SIP client or not. SIP clients answer any SIP request that is searching for any SIP ID whether the request is sent from a registrar or not [3]. A censor can probe a SIP client if it discovers its IP address [3]. Houmansadr, Brubaker and Shmatikov performed SIP probing investigations to successfully differentiate a CensorSpoofer server from a genuine SIP client [3].

Attack	Imitation Requirement	Adversary	Typical SIP clients (e.g. Ekiga)	CensorSpoofer
Manipulate tag in SIP OK	Software	LO/OB/OM	Nothing	Client closes the call
SIP INVITE to fakeID@suspiciousIP	SideProtocols, Software, Errors	LO/OB/OM	Respond with "100 Trying" and "180 Ringing", "483 Busy Here", "603 Decline", or "404 Not Found"	Nothing
SIP INVALID	SideProtocols, Errors	LO/OB/OM	Respond "400 BadRequest"	Nothing
SIP BYE with invalid SIP-ID	SideProtocols, Software, Errors	LO/OB/OM	Respond "481 Call Leg/Transaction Does Not Exist"	Nothing
Drop RTP packets (only for confirmation)	SideProtocols, Software, Network	LO/OB/OM	Terminate the call after a time period depending on the client, may change codec in more advanced clients.	Nothing

* SideProtocols = protocols that run side-by-side to the main session
** LO = Local adversary, OB = State-level oblivious adversary, OM = State-level omniscient adversary
Table 3: Distinguishing CensorSpoofer From Genuine Sip Clients (taken from [3])

5. Notable Research on Detecting Obfuscated Protocols

1. Parrot is Dead [3]

Houmansadr, Brubaker, and Shmatikov disagree that protocol mimicry is the right way to evade censorship [3]. They argue that systems like StegoTorus, CensorSpoofer, and SkypeMorph do not accomplish unobservability [3].

Several of their attacks are discussed in §4. They proved that it is possible to detect protocol mimicry without using sophisticated methods and gathering data from several nodes on the network [3]. Besides several other ways of detecting obfuscation, Houmansadr, Brubaker, and Shmatikov observed that a simple way of distinguishing a protocol obfuscation from a genuine protocol is by noting how the system responds to errors [3]. Protocol standards usually dictate how errors are supposed to be processed however a system that is creating obfuscated traffic usually cannot handle the errors the same way as it is quite an extensive job [3].

Houmansadr, Brubaker, and Shmatikov [3] perceive unobservability as the greatest requirement for censorship evasion. However, they added that it is not possible for a protocol masquerade system to completely mimic another protocol [3] due to the complex nature of protocols. They also argued that "partial imitation is worse than no imitation at all" [3]. Houmansadr, Brubaker, and Shmatikov found out that Tor is more difficult to detect than protocol masquerade systems that do not properly mimic protocols [3].

Houmansadr, Brubaker, and Shmatikov [3] recommend running a genuine protocol for achieving unobservability.

2. Seeing through Network-Protocol Obfuscation [2]

According to Wang et al. [2], researchers and activists have developed protocol obfuscation tools which "have proved to be effective in practice against existing DPI and are now distributed with systems such as Tor".

Their research showed that they could detect, with very high precision, all the protocol obfuscations, available to public at the time, by analysing small volume of network traffic data.

Obfuscation Technique	Examples	Detection	Level of Reliability of Detection
Randomizers	Dust, ScrambleSuit, and several implementations of Obfsproxy deployed with Tor	entropy + length. "Reliably detected by a combination of entropy-based tests and simple heuristics"	High
Protocol mimicry	Light weight: Format-Transforming Encryption - FTE deployed with Tor Less efficient: StegoTorus, SkypeMorph, CensorSpoofer, and Marionette	URI entropy/length. Entropy based testing. Verifying the content length. By testing "the entropy and length of the URI appearing in the first FTE-produced packet"	High
Tunnelling protocols	Meek deployed with Tor	Machine learning. Decision tree. Machine learning "classifiers trained on traffic-analysis and entropy features"	High

Table 4: Detecting Obfuscated Protocols (based on research by Wang et al. [2])

Wang et al. [2] used smart ways of finding protocol obfuscation by implementing several methods including semantics-based, entropy-based tests and simple heuristics (e.g. length checks), and testing of entropy and length of the URI appearing in the first FTE-produced packet,

3. Breaking and Improving Protocol Obfuscation [12]

Hjelmvik and John proved that statistical methods can become a very successful tool in detecting obfuscated protocols and they also observed that it is possible to fingerprint the obfuscated protocols by using the hidden information in the "statistically measurable properties" of these protocols [12]. They noted that different ways of traffic classification are Payload Examination, Social Host Behaviour, Statistical Flow Fingerprints, and Obfuscation Traffic [12].

"The SPID algorithm performs protocol identification in a TCP or UDP session by comparing the Protocol Model of an observed session to pre-calculated Protocol Models of known protocols" [12].

Two types of obfuscations are described by Hjelmvik and John.
- A payload obfuscation which makes "it impossible for a third-party to identify a protocol based on observed byte patterns in the transport-layer payload" and usually "encryption is used in order to make the payload data of a protocol appear as random while still making it possible for the recipient to restore the original message" [12];
- and flow-level obfuscation "has the goal to obfuscate statistical flow properties, such as randomizing easily observable features like packet sizes and packet inter-arrival times" [12].

As discussed in §3.4, the definitions of the two types of obfuscations presented by Hjelmvik and John above, although very well written for its time, are now deprecated.

Hjelmvik and John suggested that for improving protocol obfuscation, "payload data values in the protocols need to be randomly distributed, which can easily be achieved by applying encryption" [12]. Improvements in protocol obfuscation detection and censorship systems has improved significantly since Hjelmvik and John wrote their paper and now simply applying encryption on its own does not achieve unobservability.

Zink and Waldvogel [63] improved the BitTorrent obfuscation based on the research by Hjelmvik and John and created an obfuscation extension.

4. Predictive Modelling [83]

Work by Homem and Papapetrou [83] in the field of predictive modelling machine learning algorithms for protocol detection in DNS tunnels reveals that it is possible to detect protocols with high accuracy in real time. Not just that they successfully detected protocols but also managed to use a very small amount of available network data for determining the protocols within DNS tunnels while achieving an accuracy of 90-95%.

6. Analysis and Discussion

The goals of Protocol Masquerade process described in this study dictate that resulting traffic from protocol obfuscation and traffic morphing show the characteristics of the target protocol making the obfuscated protocol undetectable. There was only one rule behind defining the goals and that was to keep the goals simple and easy to understand. It is important to note that the optimum state in protocol masquerade can only be achieved if both goals are achieved.

Security researchers and network protocol obfuscation developers are working determinedly to build and improve network protocol masquerade systems. Their aim is to make the traffic generated by the network protocol obfuscation system look as similar to a genuine protocol as possible. Meanwhile, they are also engaged in generating traffic that mimics the genuine protocol.

Some security researchers have done phenomenal work in identifying traffic of obfuscated protocols. Remarkable research by Wang et al. [2], and Hjelmvik and John [12] proves that it is possible to detect protocol obfuscation with high precision. Although their results were extraordinary for its time but some of their work is out-dated and deprecated now. For example, their definition of obfuscation does not cover all obfuscation techniques and scenarios. They also suggested that applying encryption on its own can achieve unobservability which is not true anymore as DPIs are far more sophisticated these days.

Research by Wang et al. [2] is also very impressive. They managed to detect traffic obfuscated by all three protocol obfuscation techniques i.e. protocol randomizers, protocol mimicry, and protocol tunnelling [2].

Research by Houmansadr, Brubaker, and Shmatikov [3] reveals that protocol mimicry does not achieve the results obfuscation systems anticipate [3].

It was noted that machine learning based attacks yield highly accurate results in detecting protocol obfuscation. It was obvious that usually when a protocol is obfuscated it still possesses unique characteristics which give away the fact that an obfuscated protocol is hidden inside the traffic. Although there are many protocol masquerade systems available freely on the internet for public use, it is not hard to profile the characteristics of the traffic generated by all these systems. Such profiling data will give a nation state, an ISP, or a corporation the ability to successfully detect the protocol obfuscation.

▲ Randomizer	★ Protocol Mimicry		■ Tunnelling
System	Obfuscation Type	Has the system been attacked?	Is the traffic generated by the system detectable?
BitTorrent MSE	▲	√	√
obfs4	▲	√	√
Flash Proxies	■	√	√
eMule	▲	√	√
Freewave	★	√	√
SkypeMorph	★	√	√
FTE	★	√	√
Meek	■	√	√
StegoTorus	▲★	√	√
ScrambleSuit	▲	√	√
Dust	▲	√	√
CensorSpoofer	★	√	√
Infranet	■★	√	√

Table 5: Protocol Obfuscation Systems – Summary of systems discussed in §4

It was observed that all the protocol masquerade systems discussed in this paper have been proven to produce traffic that can be detected. Usually obfuscated traffic is detected because the traffic portrays a pattern. In most cases the pattern is very easy to discover and does not require complex and very advanced DPIs.

Censors and DPI systems are evolving swiftly. This evolution makes even the most impressive and advanced protocol masquerade systems to fade away very quickly. Some very bright ideas in the field of network protocol obfuscation never see the light of day beside the fact that they were backed by remarkable research. That is because very quickly it becomes obvious that censors can adopt very quickly and detect these network protocol masquerade systems or a research disproves the unobservability of such masquerade systems.

One of the most important aspects of a protocol masquerade system is that it should be user friendly. Many protocol masquerade systems are not easy to deploy. An average internet user who can hardly use a web browser will probably never deploy such a system. Tor browser has, to some extent, made it easier for the internet users to install and use the Tor network. However, developers of protocol masquerade systems should make sure that their systems are user friendly i.e. easy to deploy and configure and effortless to use. Some very bright censorship evasion ideas failed because they were relying on a large number of internet users to participate which never happened resulting in demise of the system. Therefore, it is important to provide user friendliness so that larger number of internet users adopt the masquerade system.

It was noted that developers of obfuscation systems are studying the previous research performed in detection of similar obfuscation systems and are improving their systems. In some cases, the previous research in detection has helped the developers of new systems to build more censorship and detection resistant protocol masquerade solutions.

7. Future Work

It is observed that most of the obfuscated protocols get detected because the traffic portrays a particular pattern or lack thereof. Automated testing tools and frameworks are required that can help obfuscation protocol designers and developers to detect flaws and unwanted patterns in the traffic generated by their protocol obfuscation systems. This will help the designers and developers to build better protocol obfuscation systems. Research is required in determining what such a testing tool or framework might look like.

Dixon, Ristenpart, and Shrimpton also noted that the obfuscation systems should be resilient to adaptive behaviour of censor and obfuscation systems should be effective even if the adversaries know the design [107]. This is only possible with constant improvement. Goals of a Protocol Masquerade process were presented in §3.4. The aim was to keep the goals simple and not to get lost in the semantics. As our understanding of the censors and detection systems improves, the goals can be extended and improved, and more goals and rules can be added in the future.

8. Conclusion

A short history of internet censorship was discussed in this study followed by an analysis of different protocol obfuscation systems.

Goals of a successful protocol masquerade system were presented. A successful masquerade system successfully hides a protocol inside a different one and adds traffic morphing to match the traffic of the cover protocol.

The investment and research that has gone into detecting obfuscated protocols is unprecedented. It is safe to assume that some countries are far ahead in detecting protocol obfuscation.

It was observed that protocol obfuscation can be easily detected with high accuracy in all systems that were studied and does not require heavy use of resources in most cases. However, as it has never discouraged the developers of obfuscation systems in the past, hopefully it will encourage them to build a truly undetectable system as one has not been developed yet. The academic research has helped developers of the obfuscation systems to improve and build better systems that are more resilient to attacks.

It is hoped that this study will help researchers and developers to design and build better anonymity and censorship circumvention systems.

9. Acknowledgements

I would like to thank Prof. Cas Cremers, my supervisor, who guided me throughout the project. I would also like to thank Dr. Andrew Simpson for helping me in the early days when the idea was in conceptual phase. Finally, a big thank you to my better half Emily without her moral support I could not have finished this dissertation.

10. Appendix A – Abbreviations & Technical Terms

Term	Meaning/Description
Cover Protocol	See Protocol Mimicry.
DPI	Deep Packet Inspection.
FTE	Format-transforming encryption.
GFW	Great Firewall of China.
ISP	Internet Service Provider
MSE	"Message Stream Encryption (MSE) is the obfuscation protocol used for BitTorrent implementations. The MSE protocol is also known as Protocol Header Encryption (PHE)." [12] BitTorrent has implemented different obfuscation mechanisms, of which, MSE is the strongest and it helps with avoidance of detection and throttling of BitTorrent traffic [50].
Mimicry Obfuscator	See Protocol Mimicry.
PHE	See MSE.
Protocol Mimicry	"A mimicry obfuscator attempts to produce traffic that looks to DPI as if it were generated by some 'benign' protocol, also called the cover protocol" [2].
PT	Pluggable transport or an obfuscator for Tor [2].
QoS	Quality of Service "The capability to provide resource assurance and service differentiation in a network is often referred to as quality of service (QoS)" [29].

	"Quality of Service (QoS) is an advanced feature that prioritizes internet traffic for applications, online gaming, Ethernet LAN ports, or specified MAC addresses to minimize the impact of busy bandwidth" [7].
Randomizers	"A randomizing obfuscator aims to hide all application-layer static fingerprints, usually by post-processing traffic with an obfuscation step that emits only bits that are indistinguishable from random ones" [2].
SIP	Session Initiation Protocol
SPID	Statistical Protocol Identification - "SPID algorithm is to reliably identify which application layer protocol is being used in a network communication session in a simple and efficient fashion." [12] and "SPID algorithm uses statistical measurements rather than relying on static pattern matching" [12].
TOR	The Onion Router.
Traffic Classification	"The concept of identifying protocols and applications through analysis of network traffic is known as 'traffic classification'" [12].
Tunnelling Protocol	"A logical extreme of mimicry is to simply tunnel data over a (typically encrypted) cover protocol. Intuitively this should provide best-possible mimicry as one is, in fact, using an existing implementation of the cover protocol." [2]
GFX	Great Firewall of X where X stands for any country or greater region.

11. Appendix B – Excerpts

Following is an excerpt from comments on "A closer look at the Great Firewall of China" page [45].

On October 9th, 2014 Anonymous said:
As a Chinese student , I don't like TorBrowser .
The TorBrowser connected slowly , and working for several minuts. Then Tor is blocked by GFW, I couldn't feel it in time.
I like Vidalia very much . It can show me the Network Map , and Advanced log.
Please release tor-Vidalia-pluggable-transports bundle as soon as possible

On October 10th, 2014 Anonymous said:
Sorry, my english isn't good enough. I love Tor , and use it everyday. Lots of thanks for developers.
I just want to say, TorBrowser is not suitable in China. The Vidalia Bundle is the best .
Because the GFW filter rules is optimised everyday , the Plugable Bridges go to failure often.
Once TorBrowser start success, after some minutes is will disconnected. It's hard to know when its down, and must restart whole Firefox, no matter how many tabs are open. So its not easy to use in China.
That's why Tor is rarely used outside CERNET. I used Tor in many city, There is no significant difference of GFW Filter between CERNET and other ChinaNets. Just because most Tor users should be Master degree or above. These guys understand Bridge, and know how to use Bridge. Other people outside univerty, mostly use GoAgent / FreeGate / Wujie etc.
According to my experience, The Vidalia Bundle is more suitable for Chinese. They user Chrome/Firefox, and install SwitchySharp/Autoproxy, and subscribe GFWList , then use Tor/Vidalia as proxy.
So, please release Tor-Vidalia-pluggable-transports bundle, following each TorBrowser release cycle.
Thanks a lot for everybody in Tor team.

On October 12th, 2014 Anonymous said:
TorBrowser does connect to the bridges. But after a few minutes, it cannot receive any data anymore. It just keeps sending data out. I need to restart the TorBrowser to make it work. It looks like the connections were closed (I do not know the exact reason, I can reproduce the simliar result by disconnecting the Internet and connect again.) But meek is exception.
some parts of china throttle non http/https connection.

Appendix B2 – Snort Rules for eDonkey [105]

Snort Distribution Rule for eDonkey.
alert tcp $HOME_NET any -> $EXTERNAL_NET 4242 (msg:"P2P eDonkey transfer";
flow:to_server,established; content:"IE3I"; depth:1; metadata:policy security-ips drop;
reference:url,www.kom.e-technik.tudarmstadt.de/publications/abstracts/HB02-1.html;
classtype:policy-violation; sid:2586; rev:3;)

Snort Rule 1000001. Rule for detection of traffic generated through eDonkey.
alert tcp $HOME_NET any -> $EXTERNAL_NET any (msg:"LocalRule:P2P eDonkey outbound
- Login Request"; flow:to_server,established; content:"IE3I"; depth:1; content:"I01I"; distance:4;
depth:1; classtype:policy-violation; sid:1000001; rev:1;)

Snort Rule 1000065. Rule for detection of traffic generated through eDonkey.
alert tcp any any -> any any (msg:"LocalRule:P2P eMule - Client to Client - Sources Request";
content:"IC5I"; depth:1; content:"I81I"; distance:4; depth:1; classtype:policy-violation;
sid:1000065; rev:1;)

Snort Rule 1000067. Rule for detection of traffic generated through eDonkey.
alert tcp any any -> any any (msg:"LocalRule:P2P eMule - Client to Client - Secure
identification"; content:"IC5I"; depth:1; content:"I87I"; distance:4; depth:1; classtype:policy-
violation; sid:1000067; rev:1;)

Snort Rule 1000068. Rule for detection of traffic generated through eDonkey.
alert tcp any any -> any any (msg:"LocalRule:P2P eMule - Client to Client - Public Key";
content:"IC5I"; depth:1; content:"I85I"; distance:4; depth:1; classtype:policy-violation;
sid:1000068; rev:1;)

Snort Rule 1000069. Rule for detection of traffic generated through eDonkey.
alert tcp any any -> any any (msg:"LocalRule:P2P eMule - Client to Client - Signature";
content:"IC5I"; depth:1; content:"I86I"; distance:4; depth:1; classtype:policy-violation;
sid:1000069; rev:1;)

Snort Rule 1000088. Rule for detection of traffic generated through eDonkey.
alert udp any any -> any any (msg:"LocalRule:P2P eMule KAD UDP - KAD Hello Request";
content:"IE4 10I"; depth:2; classtype:policy-violation; sid:1000088; rev:1;)

Snort Rule 1000090. Rule for detection of traffic generated through eDonkey.
alert udp any any -> any any (msg:"LocalRule:P2P eMule KAD UDP - KAD2 Hello Request";
content:"IE4 11I"; depth:2; classtype:policy-violation; sid:1000090; rev:1;)

Snort Rule 1000098. Rule for detection of traffic generated through eDonkey.
alert udp any any -> any any (msg:"LocalRule:P2P eMule KAD UDP - KAD2 Request";
content:"IE4 21I"; depth:2; classtype:policy-violation; sid:1000098; rev:1;)

Appendix B3 – Snort Rules for eDonkey with Obfuscation Switched On [105]

Snort Rule 1000005. Rule for detection of traffic generated through eDonkey with obfuscation.
alert tcp $HOME_NET any -> $EXTERNAL_NET any (msg:"LocalRule:P2P eDonkey outbound - Get List of Servers"; flow:to_server,established; content:"|E3|"; depth:1; content:"|14|"; distance:4: depth:1; classtype:policy-violation; sid:1000005; rev:1;)

Snort Rule 1000019. Rule for detection of traffic generated through eDonkey with obfuscation.
alert udp $HOME_NET any -> $EXTERNAL_NET any (msg:"LocalRule:P2P eDonkey UDP outbound - Status Request"; flow:to_server; content:"|E3 96|"; depth:2; classtype:policy-violation; sid:1000019; rev:1;)

Snort Rule 1000020. Rule for detection of traffic generated through eDonkey with obfuscation.
alert udp $EXTERNAL_NET any -> $HOME_NET any (msg:"LocalRule:P2P eDonkey UDP inbound - Status Response"; flow:to_client; content:"|E3 97|"; depth:2; classtype:policy-violation; sid:1000020; rev:1;)

Snort Rule 1000024. Rule for detection of traffic generated through eDonkey with obfuscation.
alert udp $HOME_NET any -> $EXTERNAL_NET any (msg:"LocalRule:P2P eDonkey UDP outbound - Server Description Request"; flow:to_server; content:"|E3 A2|"; depth:2; classtype:policyviolation; sid:1000024; rev:1;)

Snort Rule 1000025. Rule for detection of traffic generated through eDonkey with obfuscation.
alert udp $EXTERNAL_NET any -> $HOME_NET any (msg:"LocalRule:P2P eDonkey UDP inbound - Server Description Response"; flow:to_client; content:"|E3 A3|"; depth:2; classtype:policyviolation; sid:1000025; rev:1;)

Snort Rule 1000096. Rule for detection of traffic generated through eDonkey with obfuscation.
alert udp any any -> any any (msg:"LocalRule:P2P eMule KAD UDP - KAD Request"; content:"|E4 20|"; depth:2; classtype:policy-violation; sid:1000096; rev:1;)

12. Bibliography

[1]   Winter, P., Pulls, T., and Fuss, J. (2013) ScrambleSuit: A Polymorphic
        Network Protocol to Circumvent Censorship [Online]. In: *WPES '13:
        Proceedings of the 12th ACM workshop on Workshop on privacy in the
        electronic society, [Online]*. Berlin, Germany, November 04 - 04, 2013.
        New York: ACM Press, 213-224. Available from:
        http://dl.acm.org/citation.cfm?id=2517856 [Accessed 10 October 2016]

[2]   Wang, L., Dyer, K. P., Akella, A., Ristenpart, T., and Shrimpton, T.
        (2015) Seeing through Network-Protocol Obfuscation [Online]. In: *The
        annual ACM Computer and Communications Security Conference:
        Proceedings of the 22nd ACM SIGSAC Conference on Computer and
        Communications Security, [Online]*. Denver, Colorado, USA, October 12
        - 16, 2015. New York: ACM Press, 57-69. Available from:
        http://dl.acm.org/citation.cfm?id=2813715 [Accessed 12 December
        2016]

[3]   Houmansadr, A., Brubaker, C., and Shmatikov, V. (2013) The Parrot Is
        Dead: Observing Unobservable Network Communications [Online]. In:
        *Security and Privacy: Proceedings of the 2013 IEEE Symposium on
        Security and Privacy, [Online]*. San Francisco, California, USA, May 19 -
        22, 2013. Washington, DC: IEEE Computer Society, 65-79. Available
        from: http://dl.acm.org/citation.cfm?id=2498102 [Accessed 14 March
        2017]

[4]   Weinberg, Z., Wang, J., Yegneswaran, V., Briesemeister, L.,
        Cheung, S., Wang, F., and Boneh, D. (2012) StegoTorus: A
        Camouflage Proxy for the Tor Anonymity System [Online]. In: *The
        annual ACM Computer and Communications Security Conference:
        Proceedings of the 2012 ACM conference on Computer and
        communications security, [Online]*. Raleigh, North Carolina, USA,
        October 16 - 18, 2012. New York: ACM Press, 109-120. Available from:
        http://dl.acm.org/citation.cfm?id=2382211 [Accessed 24 January 2017]

[5]   BBC (2017) *WhatsApp must not be 'place for terrorists to hide' [Online]*.
        Available from http://www.bbc.com/news/uk-39396578 [Accessed 26
        March 2017]

[6]   Appelbaum, J., Mathewson, N., Kadianakis, G., Lovecruft, I., Angel, Y.
        (2017) Pluggable Transport Specification (Version 1) [Online]. *Tor's
        protocol specifications [Online]*. Tor Project. Available from
        https://gitweb.torproject.org/torspec.git/tree/pt-spec.txt [Accessed 26
        March 2017]

[7]   Netgear (2016) *How to enable Quality of Service (QoS) on routers with NETGEAR genie* [Online]. Available from: http://kb.netgear.com/24266/How-to-enable-Quality-of-Service-QoS-on-routers-with-NETGEAR-genie?cid=wmt_netgear_organic [Accessed 11 December 2016]

[8]   Moghaddam, Hooman Mohajeri (2013) *SkypeMorph: Protocol Obfuscation for Censorship Resistance*. Master of Mathematics in Computer Science, University of Waterloo, Ontario, Canada. Available from: https://uwspace.uwaterloo.ca/handle/10012/7262 [Accessed 7 November 2016]

[9]   Wright, C., Coulls, S., and Monrose, F. (2009) Traffic Morphing: An efficient defense against statistical traffic analysis [Online]. In: *Proceedings of the 14th Annual Network and Distributed Systems Symposium (NDSS)*, February, 2009. Available from: http://cs.unc.edu/~fabian/papers/morphing.pdf [Accessed 30 June 2016]

[10]   Dyer, K. P., Coull, S. E., Ristenpart, T., and Shrimpton, T. (2013) Protocol Misidentification Made Easy with Format-Transforming Encryption [Online]. In: *20th ACM Conference on Computer and Communication Security 2013: Proceedings of the 2013 ACM SIGSAC conference on Computer & communications security*. Berlin, Germany, November 4 - 8, 2013. New York: ACM Press, 61-72. Available from: http://dl.acm.org/citation.cfm?id=2516657 [Accessed 7 November 2016]

[11]   eMule Wiki (2010) Protocol obfuscation [Online]. In: eMule Wiki. Available from: http://wiki.emule-web.de/Protocol_obfuscation [Accessed 5 April 2017]

[12]   Hjelmvik, E. and John, W. (2010) *Breaking and Improving Protocol Obfuscation*. Department of Computer Science and Engineering, Chalmers University of Technology, Technical Report No. 2010-05, ISSN 1652-926X, 2010. Available from: https://www.iis.se/docs/hjelmvik_breaking.pdf [Accessed 17 July 2016]

[13]   Gustin, S. (2013) Google Unveils Tools to Access Web from Repressive Countries. [Online] Time. Available from: http://business.time.com/2013/10/21/google-digital-rebels/ [Accessed 5 April 2017]

[14]   Basin, D. and Cremers, C. (2014) Know your Enemy: Compromising Adversaries in Protocol Analysis. [Online]. *Journal ACM Transactions on Information and System Security (TISSEC)*, Article 7, vol. 17 issue 2. New York: ACM Press. Available from: http://dl.acm.org/citation.cfm?id=2658996 [Accessed 3 January 2017]

[15]   Qiang, X. (2008) How China's Internet Police Control Speech on the
        Internet [Online]. *Radio Free Asia*. Available from:
        http://www.rfa.org/english/commentaries/china_internet-
        11242008134108.html [Accessed 27 December 2016]

[16]   The New York Times (2012) *Pakistan Builds Web Wall Out in the Open*
        [Online]. Available from:
        http://www.nytimes.com/2012/03/03/technology/pakistan-builds-web-
        wall-out-in-the-open.html [Accessed 26 November 2016]

[17]   Torbati, Y. (2013) *Iran blocks use of tool to get around Internet filter*
        [Online]. Reuters.com. Available from: http://www.reuters.com/article/us-
        iran-internet-idUSBRE9290CV20130310 [Accessed 15 January 2017]

[18]   Moghaddam, H. M., Li, B., Derakhshani, M., and Goldberg, I. (2012)
        SkypeMorph: Protocol Obfuscation for Tor Bridges [Online]. In:
        *Proceedings of the 2012 ACM conference on Computer and
        Communications Security*. Raleigh, North Carolina, USA, October 16 -
        18, 2012. New York: ACM Press, 97-108. Available from:
        http://cacr.uwaterloo.ca/techreports/2012/cacr2012-08.pdf
        [Accessed 30 June 2016]

[19]   Xiong, G., Huang, W., Zhao, Y., Song, M., Li, Z. and Guo, L. (2013)
        Real-Time Detection of Encrypted Thunder Traffic Based on
        Trustworthy Behavior Association. In: Yuan Y., Wu X., Lu Y. (eds)
        Trustworthy Computing and Services. International Conference on
        Trustworthy Computing and Services 2012. Communications in
        Computer and Information Science, vol. 320. Springer, Berlin,
        Heidelberg, 132-139.

[20]   Arthur, C. (2011) *China cracks down on VPN use* [Online]. The
        Guardian. Available from:
        https://www.theguardian.com/technology/2011/may/13/china-cracks-
        down-on-vpn-use [Accessed 15 January 2017]

[21]   BBC News (2010) *Timeline: China and net censorship* [Online].
        Available from: http://news.bbc.co.uk/2/hi/8460129.stm [Accessed 10
        November 2016]

[22]   Fifield, D., Hardison, N., Ellithorpe, J., Stark, E., Boneh, D., Dingledine,
        R., and Porras, P. (2012) Evading Censorship with Browser-Based
        Proxies. In: Fischer-Hübner S., Wright M. (eds) *Privacy Enhancing
        Technologies*. PETS 2012. Lecture Notes in Computer Science, vol.
        7384. Springer, Berlin, Heidelberg, 239-258.

[23]   Basin, D., Cremers, C., and Meadows, C. (2012) *Model Checking
        Security Protocols (draft manuscript).* [Online]. Available from:

https://www.cs.ox.ac.uk/people/cas.cremers/downloads/papers/BCM201
1-modelchecking_securityprotocols.pdf [Accessed 8 January 2017]

[24]   Cremers, Casimier Joseph Franciscus (2006) *Scyther - Semantics and
        Verification of Security Protocols.* Ph.D. Thesis, Eindhoven University of
        Technology. Eindhoven: University Press Eindhoven. Available from:
        https://profs.basu.ac.ir/y-
        seifi/upload_file/cas_cremers_phd_thesis(pre_co_prj.2718.727).pdf
        [Accessed 8 January 2017]

[26]   GreatFire.org (n.d.) *When did GreatFire.org launch?.* [Online]
        Available from: https://en.greatfire.org/faq/when-did-greatfireorg-launch
        [Accessed 27 December 2016]

[27]   ProPublica (2015) *Inside the Firewall: Tracking the News That China
        Blocks.* [Online]. Available from: https://projects.propublica.org/firewall/
        [Accessed 15 January 2017]

[28]   Wikipedia (2016) *Internet censorship in China.* [Online].
        Available at: https://en.wikipedia.org/wiki/Internet_censorship_in_China
        [Accessed 30 June 2016]

[29]   Wang, Z. (2001) *Internet QoS: Architectures and Mechanisms for
        Quality of Service (The Morgan Kaufmann Series in Networking).* San
        Francisco, California: Morgan Kaufmann Publishers Inc.

[30]   Winter, P. and Crandall, J. R. (2012) *The Great Firewall of China: How it
        Blocks Tor and Why it is Hard to Pinpoint.* [Online]. USENIX; login: 37
        (6), 2012. Available from:
        https://www.cs.princeton.edu/~pwinter/pdf/winter2012b.pdf [Accessed
        29 December 2016]

[31]   Reporters Sans Frontieres (2014) *Pakistan: Upgraded censorship.*
        [Online]. Available from: http://12mars.rsf.org/2014-
        en/2014/03/10/pakistan-upgraded-censorship/ [Accessed 17 January
        2017]

[32]   Reporters Sans Frontieres (2014) *Enemies of the Internet 2014: entities
        at the heart of censorship and surveillance.* [Online]. Available from:
        http://12mars.rsf.org/wp-
        content/uploads/EN_RAPPORT_INTERNET_BD.pdf [Accessed 15
        January 2017]

[33]   Reporters Sans Frontieres (2014) *Saudi Arabia: prime centre of content
        blocking.* [Online]. Available from: http://12mars.rsf.org/2014-
        en/2014/03/11/saudi-arabia/ [Accessed 17 January 2017]

[34] Lenta.ru (2012) *The list of banned sites leaked online (In Russian)*. [Online]. Available from: https://lenta.ru/news/2012/11/12/blacklist/ [Accessed 26 November 2016]

[35] Fifield, David (n.d.) *Flash Proxies*. [Online]. Available from: https://crypto.stanford.edu/flashproxy/ [Accessed 8 April 2017]

[36] The Economist (2013) *The Great Firewall: The art of concealment (Special Report)*. Available from: http://www.economist.com/news/special-report/21574631-chinese-screening-online-material-abroad-becoming-ever-more-sophisticated [Accessed 10 April 2017]

[37] Bao, B. (2013) *How Internet Censorship Is Curbing Innovation in China*. [Online]. The Atlantic. Available from: https://www.theatlantic.com/china/archive/2013/04/how-internet-censorship-is-curbing-innovation-in-china/275188/ [Accessed 10 April 2017]

[38] Reilly, M. (2016) *Russia Turns to China for Help Building Its Own "Great Firewall" of Censorship*. [Online]. MIT Technology Review. Available from: https://www.technologyreview.com/s/602986/russia-turns-to-china-for-help-building-its-own-great-firewall-of-censorship/ [Accessed 10 April 2017]

[39] Soldatov, A. and Borogan, I. (2016) *Putin brings China's Great Firewall to Russia in cybersecurity pact*. [Online]. The Guardian. Available from: https://www.theguardian.com/world/2016/nov/29/putin-china-internet-great-firewall-russia-cybersecurity-pact [Accessed 10 April 2017]

[40] Barme, G.R. and Ye, S. (1997) *The Great Firewall of China*. Wired, issue 6. Available from: https://www.wired.com/1997/06/china-3/ [Accessed 10 April 2017]

[41] Connor, N. (2017) *China fortifies its Great Firewall with crackdown on VPNs - after Xi Jinping called for 'global connectivity'*. [Online]. The Telegraph. Available from: http://www.telegraph.co.uk/news/2017/01/24/china-fortifies-great-firewall-crackdown-vpns-xi-jinping-called/ [Accessed 10 April 2017]

[42] Brunton, F., Nissenbaum, H. (2015) *Obfuscation - A User's Guide For Privacy and Protest*. Cambridge, Massachusets, USA and London, England: The MIT Press. Available from: https://ebookcentral.proquest.com/lib/oxford/detail.action?docID=4093096 [Accessed 14 April 2017]

[43] Oxford Dictionaries (n.d.) Obfuscation. Available from: https://en.oxforddictionaries.com/definition/obfuscation

[Accessed 14 April 2017]

[44]   Grimaldi, A. (2011) *Teoxi, Mayan Prince: I. The End of Tikal.*
         Bloomington, Indiana: AuthorHouse, 379.

[45]   phw (2014) *A closer look at the Great Firewall of China.* [Online]. Tor
         Project. Available from: https://blog.torproject.org/blog/closer-look-great-
         firewall-china [Accessed 30 December 2016]

[46]   Panichas, G.E. (2014) *An Intrusion Theory of Privacy.* Netherlands:
         Springer. Res Publica, vol 20, issue 2, pp 145–161,
         doi:10.1007/s11158-014-9240-3. Accessed from:
         http://link.springer.com/article/10.1007/s11158-014-9240-3 [Accessed
         16 April 2017]

[47]   Dang, B., Gazet, A., and Bachaalany, E. (2014) *Practical Reverse
         Engineering: X86, X64, Arm, Windows Kernel, Reversing Tools, and
         Obfuscation.* Indianapolis, Indiana: John Wiley & Sons, Inc.

[48]   Dingledine, R. (2002) *pre-alpha: run an onion proxy now!.* Email to
         onion router development team, 20 September. Personal
         communication. Available from: http://archives.seul.org/or/dev/Sep-
         2002/msg00019.html [Accessed 16 April 2017]

[49]   Tor Project Wiki (2017) *Meek* [Online]. Available from:
         https://trac.torproject.org/projects/tor/wiki/doc/meek [Accessed 17 April
         2017]

[50]   Brandon, W. (2011) *Dust: A Blocking-Resistant Internet Transport
         Protocol.* [Online]. School of Information, University of Texas at Austin.
         Available from: http://blanu.net/Dust.pdf [Accessed 17 April 2017]

[51]   Köpsell, S., Hillig, U. (2004) How to achieve blocking resistance for
         existing systems enabling anonymous web surfing [Online]. In:
         *Proceedings of the 2004 ACM workshop on Privacy in the electronic
         society, WPES'04, ACM.* New York, NY, USA, October 28 - 28 2004.
         New York: ACM Press, 47-58. Available from:
         http://dl.acm.org/citation.cfm?doid=1029179.1029197 [Accessed 17
         April 2017]

[52]   Jones, B., Burnett, S., Feamster, N., Donovan, S., Grover, S.,
         Gunasekaran, S., and Habak, S. (2014) Facade: High-Throughput,
         Deniable Censorship Circumvention Using Web Search [Online]. In:
         *Proceedings of 4th USENIX Workshop on Free and Open
         Communications on the Internet*, San Diego, California, USA, August
         18, 2014. Available from:
         https://www.usenix.org/conference/foci14/workshop-
         program/presentation/jones [Accessed 17 April 2017]

[53]   Khattak, S., Elahi, T., Simon, L., Swanson, C. M., Murdoch, S. J., and
       Goldberg, I. (2016) SoK: Making Sense of Censorship Resistance
       Systems [Online]. In: *Proceedings of the Privacy Enhancing
       Technologies 2016*, vol 2016, issue 4 (Oct 2016), doi: 10.1515/popets-
       2016-0028. Poland: De Gruyter Open, 37-61. Available from:
       https://www.degruyter.com/view/j/popets.2016.2016.issue-4/popets-
       2016-0028/popets-2016-0028.xml?format=INT [Accessed 17 April 2017]

[54]   Dyer, K. P., Coull, S. E., and Shrimpton, T. (2015) Marionette: A
       Programmable Network Traffic Obfuscation System [Online]. In:
       Proceedings of the 24th USENIX Security Symposium. Washington,
       D.C., USA, August 12 - 14, 2015. Available from:
       https://www.usenix.org/conference/usenixsecurity15/technical-
       sessions/presentation/dyer [Access 17 April 2017]

[55]   Cao, S., He, L., and Li, Z. (2009) SkyF2F: Censorship Resistant via
       Skype Overlay Network. In: *Proceedings of the WASE International
       Conference on Information Engineering, 2009 - ICIE '09*, doi:
       10.1109/ICIE.2009.134. Taiyuan, Shanxi, China, July 10 - 11, 2009. Los
       Alamitos, CA, USA: IEEE Computer Society. Available from:
       http://ieeexplore.ieee.org/document/5211089/ [Accessed 17 April 2017]

[56]   Leyden, J. (2004) *Freegate is not Trojan horse, says Symantec* [Online].
       The Register. Available from:
       http://www.theregister.co.uk/2004/09/16/symantec_relabels_freegate/
       [Accessed 17 April 2017]

[57]   Dynamic Internet Technology, Inc. (2014) Freegate. Available from:
       http://dit-inc.us/freegate.html [Accessed 17 April 2017]

[58]   UltraReach Internet Corp. USA (2016) Ultrasurf. Available from:
       https://ultrasurf.us [Accessed 17 April 2017]

[59]   Wustrow, E., Wolchok, S., Goldberg, I., and Halderman, J. A. (2011)
       Telex: Anticensorship in the Network Infrastructure. In: *Proceedings of
       the 20th USENIX Security Symposium.* San Francisco, CA, USA, August
       8 - 12, 2011. Berkeley, CA, USA: USENIX Association, 459-474.
       Available from:
       https://www.usenix.org/legacy/event/sec11/tech/full_papers/Wustrow.pd
       f [Accessed 17 April 2017]

[60]   Li, S., Schliep, M., and Hopper, N. (2014) Facet: Streaming over
       Videoconferencing for Censorship Circumvention [Online]. In: *The
       Proceedings of the 13th Workshop on Privacy in the Electronic Society,
       WPES '14, [Online].* Scottsdale, Arizona, USA, November 03 - 03, 2014.
       New York: ACM Press, 163-172. Available from:
       http://dl.acm.org/citation.cfm?id=2665944 [Accessed 17 April 2017]

[61]   Angel, Y. (2015) Tor pluggable-transports/obfs4 [Online]. Available from
        https://gitweb.torproject.org/pluggable-
        transports/obfs4.git/tree/README.md [Accessed 17 June 2017]

[62]   VuzeWiki (2014) *Message Stream Encryption.* [Online]. Available from:
        http://wiki.vuze.com/w/Message_Stream_Encryption [Accessed 17 June
        2017]

[63]   Zink, T. and Waldvogel, M. (2012) BitTorrent Traffic Obfuscation: A
        Chase towards Semantic Traffic Identification [Online]. In: *IEEE 12th
        International Conference on Peer-to-Peer Computing (P2P) 2012,
        [Online]*. Tarragona, Spain, 3 - 5 September 2012. Washington, DC:
        IEEE Computer Society. Available from:
        http://ieeexplore.ieee.org/document/6335792/ [Accessed 18 June 2017]

[64]   Fifield, D. (2016) *[tor-talk] meek-google suspended for terms of service
        violations (how to set up your own).* [Online]. Available from:
        https://lists.torproject.org/pipermail/tor-talk/2016-June/041699.html
        [Accessed 22 June 2017]

[65]   Houmansadr, A., Riedl, T., Borisov, N., and Singer, A. (2013) *I want my
        voice to be heard: IP over Voice-over-IP for unobservable censorship
        circumvention [Online]*. In: NDSS Symposium 2013. San Diego,
        California, USA, 24 – 27 February 2013. Available from:
        https://www.internetsociety.org/sites/default/files/07_5_0.pdf [Accessed
        11 July 2017]

[66]   McLachlan, J. and Hopper, N. (2009) On the Risks of Serving Whenever
        You Surf: Vulnerabilities in Tor's Blocking Resistance Design. In: *The
        Proceedings of the 8th ACM Workshop on Privacy in the Electronic
        Society.* Chicago, Illinois, USA, November 09 - 09, 2009. New York:
        ACM Press, 31- 40. Available from:
        http://dl.acm.org/citation.cfm?id=1655193 [Accessed 11 July 2017]

[67]   ProtonMail (2017) *Fighting Censorship with ProtonMail Encrypted Email
        Over Tor [Online]*. Available from: https://protonmail.com/blog/tor-
        encrypted-email/ [Accessed 11 July 2017]

[68]   Hardesty, L. (2015) *Shoring up Tor - Researchers mount successful
        attacks against popular anonymity network — and show how to prevent
        them [Online]*. MIT News. Available from: http://news.mit.edu/2015/tor-
        vulnerability-0729 [Accessed 11 July 2017]

[69]   Kwon, A., AlSabah, M., Lazar, D., Dacier, M., and Devadas, S. (2015)
        Circuit Fingerprinting Attacks: Passive Deanonymization of Tor Hidden
        Services. In: *The Proceedings of the 24th USENIX Security Symposium.*
        Washington, D.C., USA, August 12 - 14, 2015. Berkeley, CA, USA:
        USENIX Association. Available from:

https://www.usenix.org/system/files/conference/usenixsecurity15/sec15-paper-kwon.pdf [Accessed 12 July 2017]

[70]   Kwon, A., Lazar, D., Devadas, S., and Ford, B. (2016) Riffle -
An Efficient Communication System With Strong Anonymity.
In: *The Proceedings on PETS Privacy Enhancing Technologies
Symposium*, 2016(2). Darmstadt, Germany, July 19 - 22, 2016. Berlin,
Germany: De Gruyter, 115-134. Available from:
https://doi.org/10.1515/popets-2016-0008 [Accessed 12 July 2017]

[71]   Illmer, A. (2017) *China set to launch an 'unhackable' internet
communication [Online]*. BBC News. Available from:
http://www.bbc.co.uk/news/world-asia-40565722 [Accessed 12 August
2017]

[72]   Haas, B. (2017) *China moves to block internet VPNs from 2018
[Online]*. The Guardian. Available from
https://www.theguardian.com/world/2017/jul/11/china-moves-to-block-internet-vpns-from-2018 [Accessed 12 August 2017]

[73]   Bloomberg News, Yang, S., Larson, C., and Ho, P. (2017) *China Tells
Carriers to Block Access to Personal VPNs by February [Online]*.
Available from: https://www.bloomberg.com/news/articles/2017-07-10/china-is-said-to-order-carriers-to-bar-personal-vpns-by-february
[Accessed 12 August 2017]

[74]   Haas, B. (2017) *China blocks WhatsApp services as censors tighten
grip on internet [Online]*. The Guardian. Available from:
https://www.theguardian.com/technology/2017/jul/19/china-blocks-whatsapp-services-as-censors-tighten-grip-on-internet [Accessed 12
August 2017]

[75]   The Telegraph (2017) *Apple removes VPN apps used to evade China's
internet censorship [Online]*. The Telegraph Technology. Available from:
http://www.telegraph.co.uk/technology/2017/07/31/apple-removes-vpn-apps-used-evade-chinas-internet-censorship/ [Accessed 12 August
2017]

[76]   Regan, T. (2017) China might not block personal VPNs after all -
The country's IT Ministry has denied a complete crackdown [Online].
Engadget UK. Available from:
https://www.engadget.com/2017/07/13/china-might-not-block-personal-vpns/?sr_source=Twitter [Accessed 12 August 2017]

[77]   Dahir, A. L. (2017) Egypt has blocked over 100 local and international
websites including HuffPost and Medium [Online]. Quartz Africa.
Available from: https://qz.com/1017939/egypt-has-blocked-huffington-

post-al-jazeera-medium-in-growing-censorship-crackdown/ [Accessed 12 August 2017]

[78]   Luhn, A. (2017) *Ukraine blocks popular social networks as part of sanctions on Russia [Online]*. The Guardian. Available from: https://www.theguardian.com/world/2017/may/16/ukraine-blocks-popular-russian-websites-kremlin-role-war [Accessed 12 August 2017]

[79]   Houmansadr, A., Nguyen, G. T. K., Caesar, M., and Borisov, N. (2011) Cirripede: circumvention infrastructure using router redirection with plausible deniability. In: *The Proceedings of the 18th ACM conference on Computer and communications security*. Chicago, Illinois, USA, October 17 - 21, 2011. New York, USA: ACM, 187-200. Available from: http://dl.acm.org/citation.cfm?id=2046730 [Accessed 13 August 2017]

[80]   Karlin, J., Ellard, D., Jackson, A. W., Jones, C. E., Lauer, G., Mankins, D. P., and Strayer, T. W. (2011) Decoy Routing: Toward Unblockable Internet Communication. In: *The Proceedings of the USENIX Workshop on Free and Open Communications on the Internet - FOCI'11*. San Francisco, CA, USA, August 8, 2011. Available from: https://gnunet.org/node/1698 [Accessed 13 August 2017]

[81]   Brooks, M. and Aslanian, D. (2009) BitTorrent Protocol Abuses. In: *The Proceedings of the Black Hat USA 2009*. Las Vegas, 25 - 30 July. Available from: http://www.blackhat.com/presentations/bh-usa-09/BROOKS/BHUSA09-Brooks-BitTorrHacks-PAPER.pdf [Accessed 13 August 2017]

[82]   Van der Sar, E. (2007) *Interview with Bram Cohen, the inventor of BitTorrent*. [Online]. TorrentFreak.com. Available from: https://torrentfreak.com/interview-with-bram-cohen-the-inventor-of-bittorrent/?doing_wp_cron=1502623430.2141339778900146484375 [Accessed 13 August 2017]

[83]   Homem, I. and Papapetrou, P. (2017) Harnessing Predictive Models For Assisting Network Forensic Investigations of DNS Tunnels. In: *The Proceedings of the12th ADFSL Conference on Digital Forensics, Security and Law*. Daytona Beach, Florida, USA, May 15 – 16, 2017. Available from: http://irvinhomem.com/pubs/2017_CDFSL_Harnessing_Predictive_Models_Forensics_DNS_Tunnels.pdf [Accessed 13 August 2017]

[84]   Feamster, N., Balazinska, M., Harfst, G., Balakrishnan, H., and Karger, D. (2012) Infranet: Circumventing Web Censorship and Surveillance. In: *The Proceedings of the 11th USENIX Security Symposium*. San Francisco, California, USA, August 5-9, 2002, p247-262. Available from:

http://citeseerx.ist.psu.edu/viewdoc/summary?doi=10.1.1.18.5049
[Accessed 16 August 2017]

[85] Khattak, S., Simon, L., and Murdoch, S. J. (2016) *Systemization of Pluggable Transports for Censorship Resistance*, ver. 2. Available from: https://arxiv.org/pdf/1412.7448.pdf [Accessed 16 August 2017]

[86] Appelbaum, J., Gibson, A., Goetz, J., Kabisch, V., Kampf, L., and Ryge, L. (2014) *NSA targets the privacy-conscious*. [Online]. Das Erste. Available from: http://daserste.ndr.de/panorama/aktuell/NSA-targets-the-privacy-conscious,nsa230.html and four subsequent webpages in the news article [Accessed 10 September 2016]

[87] Tor Project (2014) *How To: Flash Proxy*. [Online]. Available from: https://trac.torproject.org/projects/tor/wiki/doc/PluggableTransports/FlashProxy/Howto [Accessed 10 September 2016]

[88] Jarrell, Q. (2014) *Pluggable Transport Combiner Status Report 1*. [Email]. Available from: https://lists.torproject.org/pipermail/tor-dev/2014-June/006961.html [Accessed 10 September 2016]

[89] Weber, J. (2014) *Should Companies Monitor Their Employees' Social Media?* [Online]. The Wall Street Journal. Available from: https://www.wsj.com/articles/should-companies-monitor-their-employees-social-media-1399648685 [Accessed 10 September 2016]

[90] The Operator Foundation (2016) *Shapeshifter Transports [Online]*. Available from: https://github.com/OperatorFoundation/shapeshifter-transports [Accessed 19 August 2017]

[91] PluggableTransports.info (2017) *Pluggable Transport Specification Documents*. [Online], ver 2.0, draft 2. Available from: https://www.pluggabletransports.info/spec/pt2draft2 [Accessed 19 August 2017]

[92] PluggableTransport.info (2017) *History of Pluggable Transports*. [Online]. Available from: https://www.pluggabletransports.info/spec/history [Accessed 19 August 2017]

[93] PluggableTransport.info, Angel, Y., Fifield, D., Langley, A., Winter, P., and Wiley, B., (2017) *Pluggable Transports*. [Online]. Available from: https://www.pluggabletransports.info/implement/ [Accessed 19 August 2017]

[94] Cypherpunks (2017) *List of Pluggable Transports*. [Online]. Available from: https://trac.torproject.org/projects/tor/wiki/doc/PluggableTransports/list [Accessed 19 August 2017]

[95] PluggableTransports.info (2017) *Meet the Transports*. [Online].
      Available from: https://www.pluggabletransports.info/transports/
      [Accessed 19 August 2017]

[96] bLiz (2014) *Code Talker Tunnel* code on github. [Online]. Available
      from: https://github.com/blizzardplus/Code-Talker-Tunnel [Accessed 19
      August 2017]

[97] Angel, Y. (2014) *LODP* code on github. [Online]. Available from:
      https://github.com/Yawning/lodp [Accessed 19 August 2017]

[98] Author Unknown, n.d., *Pluggable Transports - Obfuscation collaboration
      web presence*. [Online]. Available from: https://obfuscation.github.io
      [Accessed 19 August 2017]

[99] Tor Project (2017) *Ticket: Allot Communications blocking of vanilla Tor,
      obfs4, and meek in Kazakhstan, starting 2016-06*. [Online]. Available
      from: https://trac.torproject.org/projects/tor/ticket/20348 [Accessed 19
      August 2017]

[100] Tor Project (2017) *Wiki: Codename: TorBirdy*. [Online]. Available from:
      https://trac.torproject.org/projects/tor/wiki/torbirdy [Accessed 20 August
      2017]

[101] OnionMail n.d. *What is OnionMail?* [Online]. Available from:
      http://en.onionmail.info/what.html [Accessed 20 August 2017]

[102] Murdoch, S. J. and Kadianakis, G. (2012) *Pluggable Transports
      Roadmap [Online]*. Available from:
      http://sec.cs.ucl.ac.uk/users/smurdoch/papers/tor12pluggableroadmap.p
      df [Accessed 20 August 2017]

[103] Flash proxy enabler n.d. Available from:
      https://flashproxy.bamsoftware.com/flashproxy/options.html [Accessed
      22 August 2017]

[104] Panait, I-C, Pop, C., Sirbu, A., Vidovici, A., and Simion, E. (2016) TOR -
      Didactic Pluggable Transport. Innovative Security Solutions for
      Information Technology and Communications. In: *9th International
      Conference, SECITC 2016*, Bucharest, Romania, June 9-10, 2016.
      Switzerland: Springer, 225-239, revised. Available from:
      https://link.springer.com/book/10.1007%2F978-3-319-47238-6
      [Accessed 22 August 2017]

[105] Freire, M. M., Carvalho, D. A., and Pereira, M. (2009) Detection of
      Encrypted Traffic in eDonkey Network Through Application Signatures.
      In: *First International Conference on Advances in P2P Systems, 2009.
      AP2PS '09*. Sliema, Malta, 11-16 October 2009. IEEE. Available from:

http://ieeexplore.ieee.org/abstract/document/5358988/ [Accessed 22 August 2017]

[106]   Geddes, J., Schuchard, M., and Hopper, N. (2013) Cover your ACKs: pitfalls of covert channel censorship circumvention. In: *CCS '13: Proceedings of the 2013 ACM SIGSAC conference on Computer & communications security.* Berlin, Germany, November 04 – 08, 2013. New York: ACM Press, 361-372. Available from: http://dl.acm.org/citation.cfm?doid=2508859.2516742 [Accessed 22 August 2017]

[107]   Dixon, L., Ristenpart, T., and Shrimpton, T. (2016) *Network Traffic Obfuscation and Automated Internet Censorship.* [Online], ver 2.0. Available from: https://arxiv.org/abs/1605.04044 [Accessed 27 August 2017]

[108]   Wang, Q., Gong, X., Nguyen, G.T.K., Houmansadr, A., and Borisov, N. (2012) CensorSpoofer: asymmetric communication using IP spoofing for censorship-resistant web browsing. In: *Proceedings of the 2012 ACM conference on Computer and communications security, CCS '12.* Raleigh, North Carolina, USA, October 16 - 18, 2012. New York, USA: ACM, 121-132. Available from: http://dl.acm.org/citation.cfm?id=2382212 [Accessed 20 July 2017]

[109]   Tails (2017) *Frequently asked questions.* [Online]. Available from: https://tails.boum.org/support/faq/index.en.html [Accessed 27 August 2017]

[110]   Tails (2017) *Why does Tails use Tor?* [Online]. Available from: https://tails.boum.org/doc/about/tor/index.en.html [Accessed 27 August 2017]

[111]   Angel, Y. (2015) *obfs4 (The Obfuscator).* [Online]. Available from: https://github.com/Yawning/obfs4/blob/master/doc/obfs4-spec.txt [Accessed 27 August 2017]

[112]   Nobori, Daiyuu (2013) *Design and Implementation of SoftEther VPN,* University of Tsukuba, Japan. Available from: https://www.softether.org/@api/deki/files/399/=SoftEtherVPN.pdf [Accessed 27 August 2017]

[113]   Tor Project n.d. *Tor: Overview.* [Online]. Available from: https://www.torproject.org/about/overview.html.en [Accessed 27 August 2017]

www.ingramcontent.com/pod-product-compliance
Lightning Source LLC
La Vergne TN
LVHW092344060326
832902LV00008B/799